Why Lawyers Should Surf

For our parents and sisters

In memory of Dr Roger Morris

WHY LAWYERS SHOULD SURF

Tim Kevan,
Barrister

Dr. Michelle Tempest
Psychiatrist

Foreword by
Barry McGuigan

© Tim Kevan and Michelle Tempest 2007

Published by

xpl publishing
99 Hatfield Road
St Albans AL1 4JL
UK

www.xplpublishing.com

ISBN 978 1 85811 386 9

Printed and typeset in the UK

CONTENTS

FOREWORD

I am delighted to have the opportunity to introduce this book by my friend Tim Kevan and Dr Michelle Tempest.

The ocean's mighty forces provide a formidable backdrop to this excellent book which is as much for the soul as it is for worldly success. There have been incredible advances in psychology and motivational techniques in recent years and this book sets them out very clearly. From my own sporting arena to those in business and the professions, anyone who is interested in improving their lot (and who isn't?) has something to learn. In this book Tim and Michelle provide a clear guide to a broad range of tools which are both easy to understand and to put into practice.

With the metaphor of surfing flowing through every chapter, what the authors have also provided is a context for these techniques, an explicit recognition of the importance of feeding the soul and listening to the whispered messages of the heart. It also allows the authors to share some of their passion for the natural world as a whole.

With this in mind I recommend this fascinating and beautiful book not only to lawyers and their employees but also to anyone else who is interested in living life with passion and to their full potential.

BARRY MCGUIGAN MBE,
Former featherweight boxing world champion,
Inducted into International Boxing Hall of Fame 2005
President of the Professional Boxers' Association

PREFACE

... and darkness was upon the face of the deep. And the spirit of god moved upon the face of the waters.

Bible, Book of Genesis

The power of the sea is manifest on many levels and we do not presume to be able to capture this here any more than King Canute could stop the flow of the tide. However, we do hope that some of the images may stoke the fires of the imagination and some of the strategies may assist on the journey through life.

Tim Kevan,
Barrister.

Dr Michelle Tempest,
Psychiatrist.

28 February 2007

Please note that this book is not intended to provide medical or other advice for particular health conditions. If you are suffering from any such condition or in any doubt, please consult a doctor before using any of the suggestions made.

Chapter 1

INTRODUCTION

I must go down to the seas again, to the lonely sea and the sky,
And all I ask is a tall ship and a star to steer her by,
And the wheel's kick and the wind's song and the white sail's
shaking,
And a gray mist on the sea's face, and a gray dawn breaking.
John Masefield

If you wander deep into the heart of legal London, past the Royal Courts of Justice, through the Temple Bar marking the entrance to the City of London and down into the Temple gardens, you will find a small statue of a little boy holding a book. It's hardly noticed even by the hundreds of lawyers who march around the gardens each day following a hearty lunch. Yet look a little closer and you see an unlikely inscription coming from nineteenth century writer Charles Lamb which resonates down the ages and is even echoed in the preface of *To Kill a Mockingbird*: "Lawyers were children once". Just as hard to believe today as it obviously was all those years ago when it was first inscribed.

It's not at all clear exactly when young, bright, enthusiastic, often idealistic people actually become "lawyers". The only thing that is clear is that it happens as sure as night follows day. The worldly air. The jaded exasperation at the over-enthusiasm of those fighting a battle for the first time. The dry, knowing look from one lawyer to another as they discuss their respective clients. Billing hours. Costs. Rain-making. Making a business out of one's most valuable commodity: time. Most of all, it comes through the use of language. The lengthy sentences. The qualifications to each assertion. The loss of the ability to admit fault.

It's not that all these changes which take place are necessarily bad. It's just that lawyers are a breed apart and you can generally spot them a mile off. With this in mind it might seem perhaps a foolish endeavour to write a motivational book for such a bunch of jaded cynics. "All that positive-thinking, American clap trap" maybe. Despite this, we hope that this book can avoid such criticisms and instead be seen as a useful introduction to some of the major innovations in the science of the mind, motivation and communication skills in recent years.

Surfing

As to the title why lawyers should surf in particular, it is hoped that this metaphor will help to illustrate some of the points made in a way which is outside of the lawyer's day to day experience. Its use has obviously become particularly prevalent in the modern world as a result of its association with computers and internet surfing. However, the connection to surfing, waves and the deep ocean beyond goes far beyond such modern inventions.

The human connection with the ocean is primeval and touches the very depths of our souls. Evolutionists might suggest that it has something to do with the fact that all species originated in the sea. Biblical references might be made to the first paragraph of the Bible which says "the Spirit of God moved upon the face of the waters", to Noah and the great flood, Moses and the parting of the Red Sea, Jonah and the whale and even Jesus himself walking on water. Psychologists on the other hand might suggest that it is due to our time in the womb or the fact perhaps that like the surface of the earth itself we are made mostly of water. As Goethe put it, "All is born of water; all is sustained by water." In *The Book of Waves*, Drew Kampion suggested that we are all drawn to the meeting of the land and the ocean because of the release of energy which happens there:

"...where ocean wave meets solid ground and gives up its accumulated life force in a powerful expression of consummation".

It is not to suggest that any of these reasons are necessarily correct, but simply that there is an almost inexplicable connection. Something which you can't quite put your finger on, yet is utterly fundamental. This connection may underlie the feeling a surfer gets when riding a wave. However, as with the connection with the ocean, the feeling in many ways diminished when one attempts to put it into words. As far back as 1777, canoe surfing was described in an account of the voyages of Captain James Cook in the following way, "I could not help concluding that this man felt the most supreme pleasure while he was driven on so fast and so smoothly by the sea".

Surfing is far more than pleasure. It is a connection with nature, the world, with God. Some might say it is love itself. It is a sense of timelessness, of other worldliness yet at the same time as connected to this world as it is possible to be. Daniel Duane describes it in *Caught Inside* as "a small occurrence outside the linear march of time". In *The Four Quartets*, T.S. Eliot describes "the still point of the turning world... [w]here past and future are gathered" and it is perhaps only in poetry and the evocation of life's mysteries that one can approach the essence of surfing with any accuracy. He goes on, "Except for the point, the still point, There would be no dance, and there is only the dance...surrounded / By a grace of sense...In the completion of its partial ecstasy."

However inexplicable it might be, the harnessing of the ocean and the mighty waves it throws shore wards provides a very powerful metaphor for the harnessing of life and everything that it throws at each one of us. On a more everyday level, it is also a sport which is away from worldly cares and to that extent contrasts with the sometimes stuffy image of the law. It is hoped that this may help to inspire the reader into seeing particular issues from a new perspective. Of course, it might also have the side effect of inspiring the occasional reader into paddling out into the waves themselves.

The book

Many of the tools and suggestions mentioned in this book will seem like common sense as soon as they have been explained. This is not to undermine their value but instead to highlight their importance. Most of us dash from one thing to the next without ever taking the time to take a step back and re-assess what we're doing. It is hoped this book will provide a framework for assessing and developing different areas of one's life and maybe along the way, even provide the odd useful suggestion. It might also be of some limited assistance in some area of a lawyer's life, even if it is only to provide a good idea as to how to bring another client through the door. Plus, it is hoped that those who read it will not be limited to the lawyers mentioned in the title as the issues covered apply to everyone, whatever their occupation. However, it is specifically written with them in mind, recognising as we have said, some of their common values, habits and goals.

The first section of this book deals with mind power and in particular provides an introduction to some powerful psychological tools which can easily be applied to everyday life. These range from re-framing to visualisations to the examination of underlying beliefs and the internal language of the mind. Such tools are best used in the context of working with others and this follows onto the next section which covers communication skills. In particular, it looks at different ways of building rapport with people through an understanding of body language and other physical and non-physical signs which we are transmitting all the time. It then goes on to give some useful guidance on various advocacy techniques which can be applied not only to help in giving presentations or lectures but also in more day to day situations where one needs to get a point across effectively.

This is followed by a section on taking action which looks in particular, at goal setting, values and ways in which positive changes can be made fast and effectively in all areas of one's life. Finally, there is a section on work/life balance and the side of oneself which keeps all else ticking, focusing on various aspects of health and leisure.

These are areas in which we are all bombarded with information everyday. It is therefore not intended as a comprehensive survey but instead to help distinguish the wood from the trees and to highlight some of the more useful things which have emerged in recent years. The book does not necessarily need to be read from front to back and it is hoped that it might also provide a checklist of useful ideas and concepts into which the reader might occasionally dip.

PART I

MIND POWER

"God grant me the serenity to accept
The things I cannot change,
Courage to change the things I can,
And wisdom to know the difference."
Attributed to Reinhold Niebuhr (1892-1971)

The power of the mind is something which is often talked about these days but still very little understood. This section of the book focuses on techniques which attempt to harness some of that power and help understand how the mind works. Ultimately, the aim is to give the reader some tools to assist in controlling the mind more effectively.

No matter what life throws at our way, as we ride the wave of life, we can still choose how to react. Life is less about what happens to us and more about what we do with what happens to us. What we do defines who we are, far more than the circumstances which are thrown at us. As the holocaust survivor Viktor Frankl, "The last of the human freedoms – to choose one's attitude in any given set of circumstances, to choose one's own way."

This section provides an introduction to some of the methods which can be used to help people change their perspective; the use of visualisation and also the power of language and beliefs to one's own moods and thoughts. Finally, it looks at how the modelling of certain characteristics of others can assist.

Chapter 2

CHANGING PERSPECTIVE

[R]iding a surf-board is something more than a mere placid sliding down a hill. In truth, one is caught up and hurled shoreward as by some Titan's hand.

Jack London

Introduction

The soul of a surfer is perhaps paradoxically carved out not during the times of great surf but instead during the times when the conditions are unsuitable for surfing. It is in these times that the surfer's true character comes to the fore, and only those with the patience and faith that surf will appear; persist and ultimately succeed. Surfers know that it is the quiet contemplative times, born of frustration, which feed the soul. This chapter is about learning from the difficult times, looking at the role that suffering can play and above all, as the title suggests, helping to change to a more positive perspective.

Why lawyers?

This book is aimed at lawyers as several studies have cited that lawyers suffer from an above average rate of low mood. In the early 1990s a John Hopkins University study compared the rates of depression among one hundred and four occupations and found that lawyers were nearly four times above the average rate of depression. This then begs the question 'why do lawyers have such a high level of depression'? There are several hypotheses for this, well beyond the explanation that law is a stressful and busy job.

Professor Martin Seligman argues that the key thing about lawyers is that they tend to have pessimistic personality types. When lawyers are asked the famous question: 'Is the cup half empty or half full?' most respond by saying half empty. This somewhat pessimistic response may be a distinguishing advantage within the legal profession, because viewing troubles as pervasive and continuing, is at the very heart of being a prudent lawyer. The inherent and honed 'scepticism skills', enable the lawyer to see every conceivable hiccup or catastrophe that might occur in legal transactions. Therefore, the ability to anticipate any pending or possible snare or disaster gives a positive legal outcome, as the lawyer can then help clients defend against potential negative eventualities. Hence, 'pervasive pessimism' and possibly 'catastrophizing' can be seen as a powerful legal tool, helping to anticipate disaster, and encouraging lawyers to think the worst before it has happened. However, on the flip side of the same coin, is that if you take that same pessimistic mindset home with you from the office, it may form part of the answer as to why lawyers are more likely to suffer with low moods.

Another hypothesis is that lawyers tend to express 'high-dominance' as a key feature of their personality; again something which aids successful legal careers. Key features of a 'high-dominance' personality include people who: interrupt others, talk longer, take charge of conversations, decide when to change topic, state strong preferences and opinions, have an unyielding manner and tend to enjoy giving instructions and advice. 'High dominance' personalities also tend to believe in statements, such as, 'winning is more important than playing the game'. This may be an integral part of being a successful lawyer who never looses a battle, however, when this is mindset extended outside the workplace it fits less well with the challenges of daily life. When things have not gone the way high dominance personalities have planned, it can be a time when they struggle to manage or cope on a psychological level.

A further hypothesis is based on the accumulating psychological evidence that much work stress arises from interacting with people rather than things. In fact, 'emotional labour' is more mentally taxing than the old fashion labour jobs that were more physically taxing. It has been shown that the more your job requires you to fake emotions, the more emotionally detached you become from those around you. Hiding or faking emotions, can lead to 'clinical burnout'. Since lawyers keep a professional detachment from their cases and cannot get too emotionally involved, this could potentially lead to the burnout state of mind. Burnout can result in symptoms of emotional exhaustion, fatigue, detached attitude towards others, low sense of effectiveness, helplessness and also low mood.

The risk of the inherent pessimism means that lawyers should be especially careful not to extend the negative mindset perspective into other areas of their lives. This book will hopefully assist the reader in finding perspective, so that even during the most difficult times in life a context can be found, which can also provide something to learn and grow from. As Shakespeare said, "There is nothing either good or bad, but thinking makes it so".

Why surfing?

If every problem is seen negatively, people very often follow the advice that it's best just to go with the flow. Sometimes for surfers, as in life, this is the answer. For example, sometimes a rip current can help take the surfer out past the breaking waves more easily. However, surfers also understand the importance of setting the right course. Just as in life, surfers need to cover the groundwork in order to get any satisfaction in the long run. The ways of the winds, the sea and its tides need to be understood. The equipment, from board to wetsuit needs to be right and then the dangers of the sea itself need to be considered. Once in the sea, surfers have to consider where the waves are breaking in order to get the best position. This might even mean paddling across a particular current to get there. They then have to choose their wave, the direction of travel and then how to ride it avoiding both rocks and other surfers in the process.

Like surfing, life is equally about making the right preparations, setting the right direction, getting into as good a position as possible and then making the choice as to which wave or opportunity to catch. In planning life's journey, forgetting the groundwork, sense of position or direction is like trying to fit together a jigsaw puzzle without having seen the bigger picture. Like the ocean, life does not and cannot stand still. Setting the right course and making decisions as to which wave to catch, helps to prevent being washed up on to the shore, or worse still on the rocks of life. Instead, surfers can help to show us how to steer our own course and ultimately follow our own destinies.

Learn from your mistakes

Perhaps even more important than having a sense of direction is how to deal with the problems which life can throw up. The way problems or setbacks are approached can mean the difference between success and failure. Surfers know their place in the ocean. They know that however good they are, the waves can be mightier. Wiping out (when a surfer gets thrown from the wave) is as much a part of surfing as gliding along the face of a perfect wave. This humility in the face of such enormous sea forces means that surfers are prepared for the worst. They know the value of the English proverb that "A smooth sea never made a skilled mariner". The value of Confucius, "Our greatest glory is not in never falling, but in rising every time we fall" and of Dr Martin Luther King, Jr, "The ultimate measure of a man is not where he stands in moments of comfort and convenience, but where he stands in times of challenge and controversy."

This was vividly illustrated by Allan C. Weisbecker in *In Search of Captain Zero* when he describes experiencing his worst wipe out in thirty years of surfing. The next day, still dripping blood from his wounds from the day before, he paddled out once again into the vicious reef break, describing not only the usual fear but always second time around, the "fear of fear". It was in facing this down and committing to continue his odyssey which showed his character and ultimately gained the respect of the local surf crew.
Ernest Hemingway knew this when he said that, "The world breaks everyone and afterward some are strong at the broken places..." Rather than wipe outs being seen as failures, they are quite properly seen as the times when most is learnt by a surfer. Perhaps they got into the wave just a little too late and went 'over

the falls'. Or perhaps they were leaning too far forward on take off and the nose pitched into the face of the wave sending them head over heels. Maybe they just misjudged the size of the wave. Whatever it was, the experience always brings another small distinction which can be made. It is the full collection of these distinctions or lessons which ultimately lead to expertise. As Buckminster Fuller once wrote, "Whatever humans have learned had to be learned as a consequence of trial and error experience. Humans have learned through mistakes."

The role of suffering

It's perhaps more than a simple act of learning from mistakes and taking different actions in the future. There is something deeper happening in times of hardship or pain. Suffering in many ways inform the soul, and whilst it is not something we would choose, it can have an important roles in our lives. In *The Problem of Pain*, C.S.Lewis said: "God whispers to us in our pleasures, speaks to us in our conscience, but shouts in our pains: It is His megaphone to rouse a deaf world". So, too, Kahil Gibran said in *The Prophet*: "Your joy is your sorrow unmasked...The deeper that sorrow carves into your being, the more joy you can contain."

Taking risks

Perhaps it is this complicated relationship between insight and suffering which allows people to take even extreme risks. Writers have for a long time described the extreme nature of surfing big waves. For example, Mark Twain explained in *Roughing It*, "It did not seem that a lightning express train could shoot along at a more hair-lifting speed." Herman Melville in *Mardi*, "Snatching them up, it hurries them landward, volume and speed both increasing, till it races along a watery wall, like the smooth, awful verge of Niagra." Jack London in *The Cruise of the Snark*, "Why, they are a mile long, these bull-mouthed monsters, and they weigh a thousand tons, and they charge in to shore faster than a man can run." Drew Kampion in *The Book of Waves* described a big wave rider as "like a matador to an avalanche".

Big waves can be described as the force of life itself. Sometimes bearing down, at other times careering us forward as if floating on air. Big waves directing us through life's mysteries. Longfellow wrote, "'Wouldst thou' – so the helmsman answered.- / 'Learn the secret of the sea? / Only those who brave its dangers / Comprehend its mystery!'" Kampion points to Rainer Maria Rilke: "We are the bees of the invisible. / We distractedly plunder / the honey of the visible in order to / accumulate it within / the golden hive of the invisible."

However, this is not to say that everyone needs to be a big wave rider. But they can teach us not to fear the unknown. To rise to the challenge and see the benefits of taking some risks. To feel alive. To realise that through acts of courage, facing fear, insight can flourish. In *You Should Have Been Here An Hour Ago*, Phil Edwards explained the need for "controlled danger" in the modern age of health and safety: "There are, as you read this, uncounted millions of people who now go through life without any sort of real, vibrant kick. The legions of the unjazzed...The answer is surfing."

Finding the perfect wave

In *Stealing the Wave*, Andy Martin describes big-wave rider Ken Bradshaw's search for *the* perfect wave "nothing real could ever match up to his imaginary, ideal wave." However, for most of us, the idea of the perfect wave can help to focus the direction which we take in life. So, how are you to recognise it? This is obviously unique for each individual and there is no easy answer. This is particularly so when one bears in mind that the brain is a complicated mixture of the conscious and unconscious. The separation between the two is similar to an iceberg; the smaller part seen above sea level is the conscious brain, and the main bulk of the unconscious submerged below the sea level. When the brain is the sum of these two parts, it is perhaps scary to think how little the unconscious mind is taken into account. One way of joining your conscious and unconscious desires is to tap into the strengths of your perfect day.

The 'Perfect Day' Exercise

Lou Reed (1972) wrote a song about his perfect day "Just a perfect day, Drink Sangria in the park, And then later when it gets dark we go home, Just a perfect day, Feed animals in the zoo, then later, a movie too, And then home". If you don't have a clear idea about your goals, then life can become a bit aimless. The 'perfect day' exercise asks you to consider what is your perfect day? So, sit down and let your imaginative and creative juices overflow. In your perfect day you have a metaphorical blank cheque, so you could be anything and go anywhere in the entire world. The key is that it is your perfect day, nobody else's and there are absolutely no wrong answers. Everyone will have a different perfect day, but you are not just thinking of a good day, but your perfect day, completely and utterly the best day ever. You should try and think about this day in as much detail as possible. The questions below may help you crystallise your perfect day:

What time would you get up in the morning?

Do you wake up alone?

What do you have for breakfast?

Would you have breakfast at Tiffany's?

Where would you be?

What do you do after breakfast?

How long is breakfast for?

Are you richer/ taller?

Then go through the day in as much detail as you possibly can. Some people may say that they are flying on Concord to pick up an award, others relaxing with their families whilst others might be catching their perfect wave. It is unique to you and can be as outrageous as you like. It is nobody else's day. It's important that before you turn the page you have a very detailed plan of your perfect day.

What does your perfect day reveal?

The perfect day exercise is the ideal way of getting the conscious mind and unconscious mind to work together, often bringing your underlying unconscious motivation to the surface. It is what you would really like to do in life and what gives you real pleasure, not what society has enforced upon you. Perhaps contrary to evolutionary psychology, sex does not usually play a big role in the perfect day exercise, although if your ideal day involved waking up with James Bond or kissing Kylie Minogue, there's no wrong day, and no two people's perfect days will ever be the same. They are as unique as fingerprints.

Happiness will probably not be achieved by replication of this exact day, but it offers the opportunity to help consider a direction of travel, helping to align your conscious and unconscious motivations. In fact, it's a bit like the so-called 'Rorschah' or 'ink blot' test, which asks you to make pictures out of ink blots, to see what the unconscious mind sees. The different images people see, come from everyone's unique brain wiring, not the ink blot shapes themselves.

With the perfect day exercise it's perhaps interesting to note that top achievers frequently do not have goal conflicts. For example, when Olympic gold medal winners are asked for their perfect day, it is often found that they will have dreamt about getting an Olympic gold on their perfect day. This shows the immense power and importance of the conscious and unconscious working in harmony. Most people find this exercise very helpful and if being a lawyer was part of your perfect day then this means you are certainly doing the right job.

Inspirations: Thomas Edison

Thomas Edison (1847-1931) was born in Ohio, USA. He developed hearing loss in childhood and became technically deaf in his early teens. He attended school for only three months and was otherwise taught by his mother and himself as his teachers felt he was not good enough for school. Despite these difficult beginnings, Edison went on to invent the phonograph, the light bulb and the motion picture camera along with many other devices which continue to affect us even today. Whilst he had natural talent, what separated him most from his peers was his positive attitude in the face of the hurdles which life throws up.

Quotations from Thomas Edison

I am not discouraged, because every wrong attempt discarded is another step forward.

I have not failed seven hundred times. I have succeeded in proving that those 700 ways will not work. When I have eliminated the ways that will not work, I will find the way that will.

Many of life's failures are men who did not realize how close they were to success when they gave up.

Genius is 1% inspiration, and 99% perspiration.

Chapter 3

MOVIES OF THE MIND

Hence in a season of calm weather
Though inland far we be,
Our souls have sight of that immortal sea
Which brought us hither,
Can in a moment travel hither,
And see the children sport upon the shore,
And hear the mighty waters rolling evermore.
Wordsworth, 'Intimations of immortality'

Introduction
Having been in the surf for a couple of hours, the image of the rise and fall of the sea and the curl of the waves is burned into the forefront of the mind and immediately appears on the closing of the eyes. It clears the mind of all the day to day troubles which may have been pressing before the session and illustrates the power which our own minds have and how they work.

Power of the mind
Many people think of exercising their hearts and muscles, but few concern themselves with exercising the brain, despite it being the focal point and the essence of the whole body. The brain has billions of inputs every day and has the mammoth task of filtering every input from its immediate surroundings, alongside deciding what to concentrate on and distilling down the information. On top of this the brain also has to compute all new information, as well as organising and maintaining an ability to recall memories and make decisions.

How the brain functions

Knowing how the brain organises information is vitally important for lawyers who are continuously dealing with the frailties of a witness memory of events. Psychologists divide the process of remembering into three stages: encoding, storage and retrieval. Encoding encompasses the initial perception of the event, storage is making a lasting record of the perception, and retrieval is recalling the event in response to a cue, such as a question. The brain can find it difficult to distinguish between what it has actually done and what it has visually imagined and this is something which is often exposed during the cross-examination of witnesses when it sometimes becomes clear that a memory was not as clear as a witness had previously believed it to have been.

Neuro-linguistic programming

NLP is the acronym for neuro-linguistic programming whose original code developers were Richard Bandler and John Grinder. This high-tech sounding name is the description given to envisaging the brain as a computer. It suggests that thoughts, feelings and actions are simply habitual and can be modified in a similar way to changing computer programmes, by deleting, uploading or upgrading a piece of computer software. Neuro refers to the nervous system and the five mental sensory pathways: vision, sound, taste, smell, and feel. Linguistics, refers to the 'silent language' of postures, gestures and habits

NLP exercises are similar to thought experiments, where the mind is the unfinished computer language and the computer programmer can create, mix and sometimes diminish neural connections. First though, how the brain creates a memory and collects information needs to be considered. Each person is different in this, so there is no need to worry if your connections are different from the next persons, as all are equally as valid. It is helpful to master the way your own 'mind's eye' works and extend this to the analogy of operating computer software.

Your Mind's Eye
The 'mind's eye' can induce emotions that are as real as if the event had just taken place. When feeling low the brain tends to focus on negative experiences and many people find themselves ruminating over bad life events. Yet, nobody would wish to watch a lousy movie repeatedly, so when feeling low, why let our 'mind's eye' play the sad memory over and over again?

Your 'Mind's Eye' Exercise
Start by thinking of a really positive life experience and ask yourself how your mind's eye recalls this memory. Try and imagine the memory and then consider how your brain replays the memory to you. To try and really understand how your brain recalls the information; it may help to jot down the answers to the following questions about how you visualise your memory:

> *Is the image still or moving?*
> *Is it colour or black and white?*
> *Is it close or far away?*
> *Is it central, or to the right or to the left?*
> *Is it in the middle of your visual field, to the side of your head or behind?*
> *Is it a silent movie or is there music?*
> *Is there talking?*
> *Is it focused or blurred?*
> *Are you dissociated i.e. do you see it as if you are an outsider watching a film?*

If you take time to really consider how your mind's eye sees memories before continuing, this will help with the exercises – as you learn to know your own mind.

Brain Images
With practice the mind's eye can be controlled in a similar way to the movie director controlling the movie scenes. If the director wants to induce sad feeling, then he has many options open to him, he may play sad music, dim the lights or show sad faces. Whereas, if the director wants to induce a feeling of happiness, he may turn up the lights, get the actors to smile, play happy music etc. The

brain is a phenomenal organ and you are more in control of your mind than the director is of any movie. You have the power to concentrate on good or bad memories and the ability to run your brain as skilfully as Spielberg directs his films.

Director of the Mind

What makes Spielberg such a successful director? What can be learnt from the master of film? It is interesting to note that Spielberg jokes that his movie career started the day he decided to jump off a tour bus at Universal Studios in Hollywood and wandered around some disused film lots. Apparently he found an abandoned janitor's closet and turned this into his office. After some time, the security guards had seen him so frequently that they would wave him through the gate. He would dress the part, looking quite professional in a suit and tie, just so he could look older than the child he actually was. By the age of twenty-one he had made his first short film for release.

Spielberg used his mental imagery and visualization at a young age to make others believe he was working at Universal Studios long before he was even offered a job. This is not to suggest that everyone should pretend to be something and someone they are not, but it does illustrate the importance of believing in oneself and one's own abilities. Spielberg believed in himself before he asked others to invest and believe in him. Now when he makes a movie, he uses the same skills of visualization on the viewer. He focuses their minds using the full cinematic experience of pictures and sounds and is able to induce feelings ranging from laugher to tears. He gets viewers' brains to concentrate on the movie, the plots and subplots and plays with the mind to attend to the nuances he desires. He uses clever psychological tricks to play with the mind and emotions.

The same skills have also helped all of the great surf explorers. As with any great endeavor, they have to be imagined as real before they can actually be achieved. So, the big wave surfer has to find the wave on the right day and visualize himself paddling into it, thinking about the potential pitfalls. He has to imagine riding down the face and his turn as he continues to ride the wave along its length. It was this sort of visualization, whether conscious or unconscious, which led Laird Hamilton and others to push forward the frontiers of big wave surfing when they started working with jet skis to tow them into waves and adding straps onto the board to keep their feet in place. As T.E. Lawrence said in *The Seven Pillars of Wisdom*, "All men dream: but not equally. Those who dream by night in the dusty recesses of their minds wake in the day to find it was vanity, but the dreamers of the day are dangerous men, for they may act on their dream with open eyes, to make it possible."

Mind exercise

Negative Image

If you think of a negative experience in your life and the image repeatedly goes round and round in your head, the image can be modified in a way similar to the way you can manipulate the image on your television screen. When you have thought of the negative image, concentrate on it, and take control of it by starting to change the image in your mind's eye. Start by turning the colour image into black and white, turning the volume down, and then down even further, until it's silent. Make the moving image slower and slower until it is motionless. Then, if you were seeing the image as if from the first person, dissociate this and look at it from outside yourself, from above. Then push the image further and further away as it becomes more disassociated. By doing this you are taking the power away from that memory, using your mind's eye to push the memory further and further away, smaller and smaller until you wave goodbye to it.

Positive Image

Next think of a happy memory and do the opposite. Turn up the volume and colour. Add smell and texture if you can. Bring the image closer and ultimately look at it from the first person as if you were experiencing the memory once again in full technicolour. We shall learn how to anchor this memory in chapter 6.

Inspirations: Rachel Louise Carson

Rachel Louise Carson (1907 - 1964) was born in Pennsylvania and had a long lasting environmental vision, which has been credited with having launched the entire global environmental movement. As an academic zoologist she was particularly concerned about the use of newly invented pesticides, especially DDT. She wrote a book entitled 'Silent Spring' which created the mental association of how pesticides aimed at eliminating one organism, still had effects felt throughout the food chain, and how what was intended to poison an insect, ends up poisoning larger animals and humans.

Quotations from Rachel Louise Carson

What I discovered was that everything which meant most to me as a naturalist was being threatened, and that nothing I could do would be more important.

We are subjecting whole populations to exposure to chemicals which animal experiments have proved to be extremely poisonous and in many cases cumulative in their effects. These exposures now begin at or before birth and - unless we change our methods - will continue through the lifetime of those now living.

The more clearly we can focus our attention on the wonders and realities of the universe around us, the less taste we shall have for destruction.

Chapter 4

LANGUAGE OF THE MIND

The voice of the sea speaks to the soul. The touch of the sea is sensuous, enfolding the body in its soft, close embrace.

Kate Chopin, The Awakening

Introduction
Rudyard Kipling described words as "the most powerful drug used by mankind." Words are the basic tool everyone uses to represent things to ourselves and then to others. Words are used internally and externally almost seamlessly to evoke messages and emotions which go with words, to empower or disempower. They are our way of describing the world around us and also of describing our innermost thoughts. They help in understanding, provoke thought and emotion and through them shape beliefs, actions and ultimately decide destiny. However, the very fact of using such man-made tools can in itself limit the experience. This was illustrated by Italo Calvino in *Invisible Cities* in which Kublai Khan asks Marco Polo why he had not talked about his home, Venice. Marco Polo replied that: "Memory's images, once they are fixed in words, are erased...perhaps I am afraid of losing Venice all at once, if I speak of it. Or perhaps, speaking of other cities, I have already lost it, little by little."

To some extent, surfers feel that way about surfing. Trying to objectify the experience into mere words, risks diminishing the feeling. It simply exposes the limitations of words themselves. To try and grasp at its essence is to grasp at thin air in searching for anything literal. Often in these circumstances it is useful to look at the origin of words, where echoes of the thoughts of past generations are found. In *Walking on Water*, Andy Martin discusses the myriad means which Lorrin Andrews provides for *he'enalu*, the Hawaiiann word for surfing, in her *Dictionary of the Hawaiian Language*. He says that it splits into two words, *he'e* and *nalu*. *He'e* means among other things, to run, flow, slip glide and also to flee as well as to ride a surfboard. *Nalu* means among other things to suspend one's judgment, to think within oneself, to search after any truth or fact, as well as the surf as it rolls in upon the beach. So, too, with the Hawaiian greeting Aloha which Drew Kampion in *Stoked!: A History of Surf Culture*, says is broken down literally as *alo*, meaning "experience" and *ha* meaning "breath of life".

It can also be useful to look to poetry as a method of evoking meaning, for example, the following words from William Blake, in many ways get a lot closer to describing surfing than simply talking about riding down the face of a wave: "To see the World in a Grain of Sand / And a Heaven in a Wild Flower, / Hold Infinity in the palm of your hand / And Eternity in an hour." This echoes' Rachel Carson who said: "In every outthrust headland, in every curving beach, in every grain of sand there is the story of the earth."

Politicians have always understood the importance of words. Churchill and Dr Martin Luther-King Jr. used the power of language to inspire people to believe in their cause. However, what is often forgotten is how important words are to each of us, both in the way we project ourselves to the world and also how we perceive our own selves. This chapter deals with the internal use of words. The later sections on communication deal with the use of language with others.

Internal language
Lawyers, above all, understand the importance of words. They are the first to object if a particular word is used against their case, which is in any way improperly prejudicial. However, the enormous effect that words can have on our own minds is often

forgotten. George Orwell summarised it in 1984 when he said "If thought corrupts language, language can also corrupt thought." The brain is like a computer with an amazing amount of Random Access Memory (RAM), but like a computer if the software is never figured out then the brain is never able to use its' own applications. If access is required to files which the brain needs to access, then the proper commands must be given to enable the use of the brain and to access its' own power. In order to get the right results we need to use the right words. Even by artificially changing the use of particular words to more positive, enabling ones, can have a profound effect on one's physiology and ultimately on the results achieved. As Confucius said, "Without knowing the force of words, it is impossible to know men".

There is a wealth of words to describe the same situation and this reflects the fact that words offer feedback for the brain about how the body has interpreted a particular situation. For example, if two people sit next to each other on a roller coaster ride, one may return saying "that was exhilarating", yet the other may report "that was petrifying". These phrases give insight into how the body has interpreted its own physiological response. The two people on the roller coaster ride both went around the same track and both experienced the same acceleration down the big dipper; yet one interpreted their physiological response as exhilarating and the other as petrifying. These words are their conscious mind describing their inner emotional state. Words are important in determining future action and may impact upon the action of others. For instance, it is unlikely that the petrified passenger would wish to go on the ride again, nor that friends would suggest that they come back another day to go on the same fairground ride.

This example illustrates the impact of words and how verbal descriptions can transform actions. It is therefore worth considering personal language used on a daily basis, and contemplating how slight changes in vocabulary may help to make daily experiences or tasks more pleasurable. By reflecting on personal internal vocabulary, it can sometimes help to change negative emotions into something more positive. For example, "problems" could be re-defined as "challenges", "annoying" might be "interesting", "confused" may be changed into "curious". A client with all of these attributes might be changed into "learning opportunity". Consider the impact of changing "Argh! I know nothing about that topic" into "I'm going to bring fresh eyes to that situation."

Artificially changing the language in this way can initially perhaps be seen as contrived and even insincere. Such criticisms do have some force, but they should not detract from the central message that words should be used carefully, not just in legal documents, but also in the message they convey to the internal mind. Calling oneself an idiot when one has done something wrong, probably won't help as much as simply forcing oneself to look at the lighter or positive side of a mistake and what can be learnt from that situation, no matter how hard that might be to see at first.

The power of internal questions
One of the most powerful tools in the language of the mind, is the use of questions. Asking the right question, can turn a situation completely around. Children learn through asking questions. However, adults often forget how important questions can be. Albert Einstein said: "The important thing is not to stop questioning...One cannot help but be in awe when he contemplates the mysteries of eternity, of life, of the marvellous structure of reality. It is enough if one tries merely to comprehend a little of this mystery everyday".

Questions can be both a help and a hindrance depending upon which ones are asked. Their use is something which lawyers, in particular, should find quite easy as it is something which they do in their jobs everyday. It is always worth asking, "what perspective may be more helpful?" and trying to change negative questions into positive ones, similar to finding an alternative route around a roadblock. So, rather than asking "is it really that annoying client on the phone again?" the question could be re-routed and asked "what else can I learn about his case by having the client on the telephone?"

Questions are important at home as well as at work. For example, in relationships people may ask questions such as, "what if the grass is greener on the other side?" Such disempowering questions only serve to fuel the fire of doubt and discourage commitment. Compare this to asking a question such as, "How nice can I be to the person I love today?"

The turning it around exercise
Think about a difficult or challenging situation which you are currently facing or have recently had to deal with. Then ask the following questions and see if it helps in any way.

1.   *What is positive about this situation?*
2.   *How might I change the way I am looking at this?*
3.   *What does it teach me for next time?*

For examples of other empowering questions, see chapter 10.

The power of internal metaphors
Most people receive information or factual input, by using a visual mind map. This means that one of the best ways for passing on messages is to paint a picture in another persons' mind. This is how information was passed on in the days before books; stories were told and imparted down from one generation to the next. Jose Ortega y gasset said, "the metaphor is perhaps one of man's most fruitful potentialities. Its efficacy verges on magic, and it seems a tool for creation which God forgot inside one of His creatures when He made him." How much better, for example, to take the poet Rabindranath Tagore's description of the Taj Mahal, a monument to the Emperor Shah Jahan's wife, as "a teardrop on the cheek of time", than merely to describe its physical appearance?

The importance of the metaphor applies equally when examining the way in which you communicate with yourself. For example, "I'm struggling to keep my head above water", is a cry many lawyers have howled under the pressure of work. But consider what this powerful metaphor is creating internally. Ultimately internal stress increases as the brain has visions of gulping and gasping for air as the lungs fill with water.

Therefore, instead of giving a drowning metaphor perhaps try saying "I'm riding the wave of life". Then follow this metaphor and explore what else it is conveying. On examining this metaphor it informs the wave rider that they have had to work hard to get into the right place to catch the wave in the first place. They paddled hard to catch the wave when it arrived, and caught it through sheer commitment to the purpose. They glided down the face of the wave, perhaps elated to be there. But before long, they'll have to change direction, to make a bottom turn to continue else the wave will simply close out in front. Perhaps there's a fast section ahead where simply holding on will allow adrenalin to carry them through. After that there might be a little more time when they can have a look around, perhaps even do one or two manoeuvres. Then, just as it's all going right the wave might start to close out ahead and unless they do something pretty radical the ride will end. The surfer could travel up to the lip of the wave and turn sharply gaining speed and momentum and might just squeeze through the section of wave. Then, ahead, the lip might be curling over. The surfer might stall the board a little and hit...perfection. Inside the tube. Surrounded by water. Everything in the world as it should be. Transcending time. The moment cherished. Then they'd be flying out and into the open air, onto the next part of the wave which might be smooth, tranquil. Time for a breather on the wave of life.

It doesn't matter what metaphor you choose so long as it is an empowering one. If working is seen as akin to "pulling teeth", it will make the task feel much more arduous than if it was seen as "playing a game". Or if you are seeing life as "a quagmire", try viewing it as "a beach".

So, above all, it's important to remember that with every metaphor the brain is also receiving an internal message. It's far easier supporting the mind than holding it back with the use of metaphors such as drowning or pulling teeth.

Mother Theresa understood this when she said the following:

Life is an opportunity, benefit from it.
Life is a beauty, admire it.
Life is a dream, realize it.
Life is a challenge, meet it.
Life is a duty, complete it.
Life is a game, play it.
Life is a promise, fulfil it.
Life is sorrow, overcome it.
Life is a song, sing it.
Life is a struggle, accept it.
Life is a tragedy, confront it.
Life is an adventure, dare it.
Life is luck, make it.
Life is life, fight for it!

Inspirations: Rosa Parks

Rosa Louise McCauley Parks (1913 - 2005) was born in Alabama and was an African American seamstress who the U.S. Congress dubbed the "Mother of the Modern-Day Civil Rights Movement". Parks is famous for her refusal to obey a bus driver's demand to relinquish her seat to a white passenger. Her subsequent arrest and trial for this act of civil disobedience triggered the Montgomery Bus Boycott, one of the largest and most successful mass movements against racial segregation in history.

Quotations from Rosa Parks

People always say that I didn't give up my seat because I was tired, but that isn't true. I was not tired physically, or no more tired than I usually was at the end of a working day. I was not old, although some people have an image of me as being old then. I was forty-two. No, the only tired I was, was tired of giving in.

I did not want to be mistreated... I had not planned to get arrested. I had plenty to do without having to end up in jail. But when I had to face that decision, I didn't hesitate to do so because I felt that we had endured that too long. The more we gave in, the more we complied with that kind of treatment, the more oppressive it became.

Chapter 5

BELIEFS

Whenever I find myself growing grim about the mouth; whenever it is a damp, drizzly November in my soul ...then, I account it high time to get to sea as soon as I can.

Herman Melville, *Moby Dick*

Introduction
If the ocean is the earth's heart, then the tides are its steady beat. Surfers spend hours sitting on their boards rising and falling with the waves and marching to and from the surf in time with the tides. It is no wonder then that many describe surfing as itself a religion. In fact, one of the fathers of modern surfing, Tom Blake, described nature as God. Others say that nature is a revelation of the glory of God. Whatever one thinks, it is right to say that very few of us believe in nothing at all, even atheists know what they don't believe in.

On a smaller scale there are numerous beliefs held, some of which empower and some of which do not. This chapter examines the effect which beliefs can have, often without even realising.

What is a belief?
Many mainstream psychologists think that beliefs are the building blocks of conscious thought. Beliefs can be seen as the foundations and frameworks of understanding, analogous to the building of a bridge where beliefs sit upon the pillars of facts. Therefore, the power which beliefs have is enormous, as they can affect the direction of personal choice and ultimately the route of lives.

Eliminating disempowering beliefs

As beliefs are so important in decision-making, it is crucial to examine our own underlying belief system and what our invisible guides really are. Many people are surprised to find that they possess numerous very negative underlying beliefs, which without a great deal of effort can be challenged and even eliminated.

Beliefs exercise: changing disempowering beliefs

In order to challenge negative beliefs and work out which beliefs are holding you back, try and think of the principles you adhere to, or perhaps which you repeat after something goes wrong, which on reflection aren't terribly positive. Examples might be the following:

> "Bad things are always happening to me."

> "I'm just an unlucky person."

> "I always lose."

> "It's always me."

> "I don't like to do things which I'm not already expert in."

Once you've pinpointed say five such beliefs, try and think of an alternative belief which would be more positive. Although it may seem contrived, it is surprising what effect the simply swapping of such small beliefs can have on one's life. Often, they can help to take away one's limitations or can assist in facilitating a more positive attitude to all situations.

Empowering beliefs

Everyone is made up from a multitude of beliefs and it is in no way suggested that these should all be tinkered with. However, it is instructive to take examples of beliefs which can be of assistance. The following provides merely some small examples of such beliefs taken from the surf.

Money is not the route to all happiness

Some people say that wealth brings happiness; yet others who are as poor as a church mouse financially, still feel fulfilled. In fact, large cash lottery winners have not been found to be any happier than victims of a car crash, six months after the life event.

Psychologists have shown that the four hundred richest Americans when compared to the Maasai of East Africa, have very little difference in their happiness levels, yet vast differences in monetary terms. It is often the smaller things in life which relate more to happiness than wealth. One might say that the stereotypical surfer is generally happy and this may be because instead of concentrating on money, the surfer views the world itself as a rich place with a full appreciation of the beauty of the surrounding natural world.

Happiness comes with gratitude

When Tom Blake was seventy seven years old, the surf pioneer wrote the following (later re-printed in The Surfer's Journal), "Everything sparkles with new life and vitality, including my antiquated body." He was eternally grateful for the gifts he was offered each and every day. This is something most of us forget much of the time. In a consumer-driven society where "the customer is always right" we tend to expect things to go right and therefore take many of the small things for granted. Exercising gratitude is all about appreciating the things you have in your life. It is a way of reaching back to your inner happiness and it allows you to notice what is right instead of just what is wrong.

One useful exercise to undertake at any time when you are feeling particularly challenged, unhappy or unsettled is to list ten things you are grateful for in your life, including things you usually take for granted. This could include your health, family, home, friends and work colleagues. After that add to the list all things you could not survive without, such as air, water and food. Take time to focus on these wonders. Look at these things as if you were doing so for the first time. Go outside, slow down and appreciate the natural beauty around you and begin to enjoy the simple things in life, such as walks and sharing meals. Become aware, every second, of just how much joy there is in your life. Say 'thank you' as often as possible to all the people who make your life what it is. Adopt gratitude.

You reap what you sow

In Buddhism, the Buddha is reported as saying "if you knew what I know about the power of giving, you would not let a single meal pass without sharing it in some way." Whether it be through the notion of karma, the cause and effect in Buddhism, Hinduism or the Christian notion that you reap what you sow (eg Psalms 126:5: "They that sow in tears shall reap in joy") most religions are agreed on the benefits to the spirit of sacrifice, of giving and sharing. Robert Louis Stevenson said, "Don't judge each day by the harvest you reap, but by the seeds you plant." Surfers understand this. When they are in the line-up waiting for waves, it is absolutely crucial that they share. Without this spirit of generosity which is prevalent among most surfers there would be accidents and a bad atmosphere, which would completely defeat the purpose of being there.

In society as a whole, perhaps the most valuable thing which people give is their own time to help others in one form or another. Others give money via tithing, by the giving of a tenth of their income. In the current consumer society it is important not to forget the value of things other than material goods. It sounds obvious, but it is nevertheless often over-looked. When one particular material aspiration is fulfilled, it is replaced with another, this is similar to what psychologists call being caught on the 'hedonistic treadmill'. No matter how fast you spend, you will never catch up with your expectations. The experience of always wanting more and living for the future, always rushing to the next rung of the ladder without stopping to reflect on what you already have, can lead to dissatisfaction. It's a bit like being a plant perpetually in flower; without allowing for a change it quickly wilts and dies, never enjoying all four seasons.

Mistakes are opportunities for discovery
Gary Emery, an American cognitive therapist said "if a thing is worth doing it is worth doing badly." James Joyce described mistakes as "the portals of discovery" and if you stop punishing yourself for mistakes and instead take on board the lessons, you will find a way to prosper even in misfortune. Surfers know that it is through falling off the board and wipe-outs that they very often make the most progress. Once you have learned the lessons from the mistake, the next trick is not dwell on the negative aspects of the mistake, but instead to ensure that you have learnt the lesson which may have arisen as a result of the mistake.

Taking responsibility is a mark of strength
One of the premises of cognitive analytical therapy is to understand how you can be a good parent to yourself. Within that role comes taking responsibility for your own actions and mistakes. By respecting yourself enough to be your own responsible parent you also develop your unconditional love along with the understanding that nobody is perfect, everyone makes mistakes. In one of the recent issues of Surfer's Path, the editor Alex Dick-Read described how he was injured when he accidentally dropped in on another surfer. Though entirely unintentional, he took responsibility and rather than sweeping the incident under the carpet, he not only owned up but did so in his editorial to the world. The humility and pathos which flowed from this transformed the article and forged a much closer connection with the reader. It was a classic example of the principle that to take responsibility is a mark of strength. This is something that lawyers in particular need to be aware of as they often find it difficult to admit any fault whatsoever, perhaps because their instincts are to admit nothing unless they have to.

Focus on the solution
Surfers know that if they are going to catch the waves they want, then they have to focus on the way they are going to do it, not on all the difficulties which might ensue. This is not to suggest that one should ignore such possibilities but it is to suggest that you try and avoid getting bogged down with them. A good rule of thumb is to try and spend around 90% of your time focusing on the solution leaving only 10% worrying time about the possibility of

failure. Do not be distracted by others who have succumbed to the same failure, even though this may seem comforting. Instead start focusing on successful solutions and never see failure as permanent, only as transient.

Smiling cheers you up
Whether it's a wry smile after falling off a perfectly peeling wave or a satisfied smile after a long ride, surfers know the benefits of humour, optimism and cheerfulness. However, even a forced smile can have a positive effect on one's mood. Try, for example, pulling the sides of your mouth up in the shape of a smile and holding it for twenty seconds. To the average person this may seem very silly yet often it can tangibly improve one's mood. Making the shape of a smile uses the muscle groups in your face that connect with a particular pattern of brain activity. Because the brain links these areas, a chain reaction is set up in between the movement of your face muscles and the pattern of activity within your brain. This chain reaction induced is associated with positive happy feelings in your emotional centres. Because cells that 'wire together fire together' and by activating the wires that cause a smile, they fire links to positive emotions. So just by moving your mouth into a smile causes a small increase in positive emotion related brain activity.

Congruency
On a deeper level, when one looks into what makes people happy, one factor is whether people are making an effort to try and live in accordance with their underlying beliefs and values. This is all a matter of degree rather than absolutes, but when values are completely out of line with actions or internal beliefs, there is a risk that this dichotomy can lead to internal tension and ultimately unhappiness. One of the issues of congruency for lawyers is taking on too many cases and working long hours, whilst also trying to balance family and friends. For surfers it may be the tussle between getting into the sea frequently enough whilst also having enough time for family and a job. This is different for each person and requires people to look inside themselves and ask what drives them and what makes them happy. In Gift from the Sea, Anne Morrow Lindbergh said, "I am seeking perhaps what Socrates asked for in

the prayer from Phaedrus when he said, "May the outward and the inward man be at one.""

Congruency exercise
Whilst most of us have values in one form or another, many do not know quite what they are, and it is a useful exercise to try and identify them. In order to assist in this, try writing a list of the core values that are most important to you. Then write down five situations in your life when you truly felt congruency between your values and actions. Reflect on what was going on in detail. What core values were you expressing?

Once you have identified these core values, list five things you could do over the next week, to bring these further into your life. Then list five areas where you feel that you are currently not living in accordance with your values and write down five suggestions that you might try in the next week to improve this situation somewhat.

Inspirations: Dr. Muhammad Yunus
Dr. Muhammad Yunus, was born in 1940, the third born of 14 children in Bangladesh. As a banker and economist, he developed the concept of microcredit, the extension of small loans to entrepreneurs, too poor to qualify for traditional bank loans.

He first got involved fighting poverty during the Bangladesh 1974 famine. He discovered that a very small loan could make a disproportionate difference to a poor person. His first loan consisted of $27 US from his own pocket, to a women who made bamboo furniture. Traditional banks were not interested in offering her such a tiny loan. However, he found that by loaning money, with very reasonable interest rates, she was able to finance her entire family. His revolutionary discovery was that by loaning money, rather than just giving money, he discovered the cycle of poverty could be broken.

In 1976, Yunus founded the Grameen Bank (Grameen means "of rural area", "of village") to make loans to poor Bangladeshis. As it has grown, the Grameen Bank has also developed other systems of alternate credit that serve the poor, such as offering education loans, housing loans, financing for fisheries and irrigation projects, venture capital, textiles, along with other activities. In 2006 he and the bank were jointly awarded the Nobel Peace Prize, 'for their efforts to create economic and social development.' The Grameen model of micro financing has been so inspiring that it has been emulated in twenty three other countries.

Quotations from Dr Muhammad Yunus
Whilst he was teaching in Bangladesh, the country was in famine and he said:

> *I was teaching...and feeling helpless. I teach beautiful theories of economics, and people are going hungry...Forget about those theories. I'm a human being, I can go and touch another person's life.*

He advocated that by fixing poverty, you are also attacking a root cause of terrorism.

> *We must address the root causes of terrorism to end it for all time, I believe putting resources into improving the lives of poor people is a better strategy than spending it on guns.*

Chapter 6

MODELLING AND ANCHORS

For whatever we lose (like a you or a me)
It's always ourselves we find in the sea

E.E.Cummings

Introduction

Once you've got a grip on each of the aspects dealt with in the preceding chapters, the internal perspective, movies, language and beliefs, you can start and see things in the context of society as a whole and how we all interact with each other. You can start to see the importance of the fine distinctions and choices which you make on a daily basis and how these can affect you and others. This is analogous to the time when surfers have learnt the theory of how waves work and perhaps how to stand up on a board whilst still on the beach and they then can get in the water and put the theory into practice. Surfing from the perspective of the ocean itself rather than merely looking out from the safety of the land.

This chapter deals first with the concept of modelling, the copying of certain traits in others which have proved successful. It then goes on to look at how advertising and other subliminal messages can affect our minds and finally, it examines how it's possible to learn to anchor the positive changes to give them long-lasting effects.

Modelling

As mentioned above, modelling is the copying of certain behaviours of others which have proved successful, a short-cut in many ways to the end goal. It involves looking around for role models and picking out the key characteristics which make those people what they are. In the surf, as in life the role model is often quite easy to find. The surfer effortlessly paddling out, arriving at the right spot as if by instinct and then catching the right wave back in again. Someone for whom, it all seems to be going right. However, this image of ease often belies numerous distinctions and much hard work which have gone into getting to that position. It is this that we need to concentrate on. To learn those lessons, as early as possible, and make the changes the easy way. However, before looking at the mechanics of modelling, it's worth examining some of the theory behind it to show why it works in practice and also to look at what happens when we blindly follow bad role models.

Nature and nurture

The human brain develops long after nature's unique genetic code has been allocated and subsequent embryonic growth. The brain continues with the capacity and the necessity to develop and learn via nurture. Children learn their behaviour and coping strategies, in part, by copying and mimicking. Learning from people around them; parents, siblings, friends and society in general. Brains therefore develop as a conglomeration of an infinite source of memories; a bank of situations that you and those around you have found themselves in and how those situations were dealt with.

Imitation and reinforcement

According to social learning theory, behaviours are part learned by imitation of others and via reinforcement, progressively built upon. In fact, throughout life each social situation is uploaded into the brain and the brain has the potential to lay down, modify or reinforce its own hard wiring. Hence, the information the brain gets given is important and perhaps especially so whilst children, as the child's brain is very rapidly developing social hard wiring.

The doll experiment

This example really brings home just how imperative it is to understand the impact of brain inputs. Back in 1965, Bandura and others actually demonstrated that behaviour can be influenced directly by brain inputs. They investigated how children's aggressive tendencies can be influenced through imitation and vicarious learning. A study was devised using 'observational spontaneous learning'. Three separate groups of children were shown a film about an adult behaving aggressively towards a child-sized doll. The first group watched the video of an adult kicking, pummelling and punching the doll. Another group watched the same video but at the end of the film they saw another adult actually praising the aggressive behaviour, by offering sweets and lemonade. The final group saw the same video but at the end they saw another adult scolding the aggressive behaviour and warning against further aggression.

Following the film all the children individually went into a playroom filled with toys which included a child-sized doll and the number of imitative aggressive acts was recorded. It was found that the group of children who observed the video including a warning against aggressive behaviour, performed far fewer observed violent acts than the children who had not seen any negative consequences for the aggressive behaviour or the children who had seen bad behaviour praised. This simple experiment illustrates the importance of brain inputs and the subsequent influence on the brain. This case illustrated the negative effect that modelling the wrong behaviour can have.

Television violence
Such effects are also commonly believed to occur after increased exposure to television violence, as there is a reduction in the emotional response to violence, as brains become 'desensitised' to viewing on-screen violence. This leaves a potential problem for both viewers and film-makers. Film-makers need to escalate behaviour in order to get the same level of emotional response, whilst the viewer develops desensitisation to viewed violence. A study in 1974 by Drabman and Thomas found that eight year olds were less likely to tell an adult about a fight in the playroom after viewing a violent programme than if they had not seen it. The ongoing debate about the relationship between media violence and aggression is far from resolved. In Britain the link between the two was brought back into the spotlight following the murder of two year old James Bulger by two teenage boys in 1993. At their trial, Mr Justice Moreland said "It is not for me to pass judgement on

their upbringing, but I suspect that exposure to violent video films may, in part, be an explanation."

Brain hygiene
Whatever the precise answer to these issues, there is little doubt that the continual inputs the brain receives from the outside world are important factors in shaping decisions and actions. Lawyers in particular are aware of this, as they take great care to ensure that any information given to the jury is not improperly prejudicial. Likewise, lawyers advise the media on what they are able to broadcast about on-going cases so as not to undermine the right to a fair trial and to avoid being in contempt of court. Hence, the legal profession are acutely aware of the effect which information can have on the mind. It is these skills which they can use when considering the importance of reviewing their own brain inputs for, as part of a healthy lifestyle, brain hygiene is something which can be included.

On a more political level, there is the issue as to whether the media itself should actually regulate some of the messages it sends out, given the power which role models can have on people's lives. This has recently come to the fore in the debate about advertisements using underweight models and whether this actually changes societies view as to what is normal or not, and what effect this can have on the vulnerable. There is growing concern that eating disorders, such as anorexia nervosa have become far more prevalent in the West, in countries which glamorise an unhealthy body image. Influences and trends within society can shape internal beliefs and expectations. What develops is a kind of 'collective culture', or 'that's the way things are done around here.' This may well be setting ourselves up for inevitable failure, if role models embedded within the 'collective culture' are stereotyped but unrealistic. It's important not to confuse advertisements with life and to be able to step back from all consuming unhealthy brain inputs.

Modelling Behaviour Exercise
Since behaviour is learnt, many people like to blame their parents for their maladaptive coping strategies, and this in part may be true. However, this also provides good news; if behaviour is plastic then it can also be modelled. Behaviours can be learned, changed

and modified. The door is therefore open to breaking the cycle of destructive coping mechanisms and instead turning to positive and adaptive alternatives. After all, you can choose which behaviours you copy and model.

You may wish to think of an effective role model, perhaps an individual who seems to have things right in a particular area. Perhaps it is time management, legal knowledge or even just office politics. Whatever it is, analyse what that person does in that particular area of their lives. Look at the way they go about it in detail and make a list of the distinctions which they are making, and which you are not. Then, one by one, try implementing some of those traits into your own life and see the difference that they can make.

As mentioned above, surfers can do this by watching the best surfer in the sea. However, just as at work, surfers can go one step further. They can pick out the best in the world and analyse exactly what skills those people have developed in order to surf the way they do. More than that, they can analyse how that particular surfer got to where they are now, the path they had to take. Along any journey, the traveller is learning from his mistakes and if you, the viewer, can also learn from that person's mistakes, as well as his successes, it is like taking a significant short cut on your own journey. Once you've made your analysis, copy the details you have noticed. Model them until step by step you find that you start to take on some of the actual qualities of that other person.

Self-visualisation

Once you've successfully modelled, visualise yourself performing a particular task. Go through every detail and imagine you are doing it at that precise moment. Feel how it would actually feel. In his description of the world's most ferocious break, Banzai Pipeline, Sam Moses describes surfers doing exactly this: "Surfers are rarely so reckless as to charge into the tubes without watching them for a while – mind surfing, they call it…"

Re-framing and association

As well as realising the influence that other people's behaviour can have on our own, it is also important to realise the importance that other societal influences can have. It's necessary first to examine some of these in order then to work out how we can channel these types of influences in a positive direction and learn to anchor them in our minds.

Advertising

One of the biggest influences in this respect is advertising which is a multi-billion pound industry employed to frame and re-frame our perception of different products. Companies tussle for position in our brains, wanting us to associate their logo with everything that is desirable. It is an intriguing point of reference to consider how the marketing industry tries to manipulate the psychology of a population. Their success and failure stories can teach us a great deal, not just about advertising, but about how brains receive and processes information.

In the early 1900s Walter Dill Scott wrote some of the first books on advertising. The most fundamental principle he identified was that of 'association'. Adverts aim to associate the product well beyond a mere logo. Very often, they aim for an association with a whole lifestyle. One of the most successful advertising slogans in surfing history is Billabong's enigmatic, "Only a surfer knows the feeling". They tapped into all of the essence of how it felt to be a surfer, rather than merely concentrating on the products they were selling.

Even political parties are now in on the act. First, it was the New Labour re-framing as modern, centrist. Now David Cameron's Conservatives are leading the change re-framing or re-branding themselves as centrist, socially responsible environmentalists. Even the logo has been redrawn and replaced by a 'tree'. Some claim the Conservatives are now more about an aroma, trying to re-frame themselves within the modern lifestyle rather than creating new policies. Others suggest that there is little difference between re-framing and political spin. However, there is little doubt that the message a brand associates with has important implications.

Subliminal messages

By far the most controversial aspect of advertising is subliminal advertising. It originated in America when market researcher Jim Vicary arranged for the owner of a cinema to portray messages, during a movie, so quickly, or printed so faintly, that they couldn't consciously be perceived other than via 'subliminal perception'. The messages 'Hungry? Eat Popcorn' and 'Drink coca-cola' were found to increase sales of popcorn by about 50% and soft drinks by 18%. Despite subliminal messages being made illegal in the 1950's, they have recently been making a comeback. In an American department store, music was mixed with a barely audible and rapidly repeated whispering of "I am honest. I will not steal" after which there was a reported a dramatic decrease on shoplifting. However, in a study in 1991, Zimbardo and Leippe found that so far "none of the more fabulous claims for subliminal marketing have been borne out by well-controlled and replicable studies".

De-junking

Just as the shorelines of the world are constantly being pummelled by crashing waves, so we are bombarded with messages each day. The brain is constantly processing and filtering information as it arrives and packaging only a limited amount onto our conscious, the rest, like the subliminal messages, going into the unconscious. They also show that just as advertising companies can change our spending habits by the messages and associations they send to us, so we can do this for ourselves by creating positive messages and associations in our own minds and de-junking the negative ones.

The way we go about re-framing our own minds is to look at some of the factors which we have analysed in the preceding chapters. Changing perspective, performing visualisations and examining our own words and beliefs. However, the risk is that some of the changes which one can make may only be short term unless they are anchored properly in the brain. This is something which advertising companies in particular have excelled at.

Perhaps it is one of the great attractions of the deep ocean. That we are away from all human influences we are at one with the world. Perhaps this is what Joseph Conrad was getting at when he said, "The true peace of God begins at any spot a thousand miles from the nearest land".

Anchors

Whilst one of the best ways to anchor any behaviour is through repetition, there is a short cut to this which has often been exploited by advertising companies and that is anchoring. So, just as a ship risks being blown onto the rocks if it is not properly anchored, so it is with the various associations and re-wiring we can do to our brains unless they too are anchored, given some permanence.

Anchoring is a way of hard-wiring the brain, of short cutting between two associations. Advertisers will do this, for example, by showing you a picture of the perfect wave, triggering the feeling of pleasure for any surfer and then putting a picture of their particular surf gear at the side. Eventually, just by seeing the surf gear, your brain gives you the same feelings as if you were looking at the perfect wave.

Ideally an anchor is similar to the pressing of a button to create a physiological state that you acquire without having to think about it. This is similar to the famous Pavlov dogs, salivating each time they heard the sound of a bell. Unfortunately, most of us have developed anchors haphazardly. However, we do have the ability to create our own personal positive anchors.

Exercise to create your anchor

In order to create an anchor, you need to start with two things:

1. First of all, you need to think of a memory of a particularly special time when you felt good, positive, strong and successful. For a surfer this may be catching the best ride in their life. Remember the way you felt and how your entire body and whole physiology felt at the time. The more intense the physiological state the easier it is to anchor. The mind and physiology need to be congruent, as the body and mind must be working together in harmony.

2. You then need to choose a unique stimulus which you can start associating with the memory and all the empowering feelings which it engenders and ultimately which will

simply start triggering those feelings by themselves. It might be, for example, to squeeze one of your hands into a tight fist. Alternatively, it might be the saying of a particular word or catch-phrase to yourself.

Now you have the tools the next step is to anchor the two together, to hot-wire them together into direct association. You will need to practice this repeatedly for the brain associations to develop the anchor. So, in a quiet room with no distractions think of your empowering memory, the time when you were feeling 'on top of the world'. Remember it in minute detail. Maybe for the surfer, the face of the wave is opening up, the sun is setting, the breeze just slightly off-shore. Maybe a porpoise or a seal had just been playing nearby. It might even be warm water on that perfect day.

You can go even further if you like and start looking more deeply at the experience. For example, in The Book of Waves, Drew Kampion described how, "The wind speaks the message of the sun to the sea, and the sea transmits it on through waves. The wave is the messenger, water the medium." So, the sun warms the earth creating the winds which ultimately create the waves which surfers eventually try and catch as they crash to shore. Thoughts such as these can only enhance the memory, provide it with added context.

Then, back to the memory itself, get your mind to replay it. Make it bright and clear. If there is light and colour, turn them up, if there is sound, turn up the volume. Put yourself in the first person so that you are experiencing it first hand. As you remember the memory in detail, your physiology and emotions should be repeating the way you felt during that wonderful experience. At the peak of the 'feel good factor' you should do the action you have chosen, for example squeezing a particular fist.

This will take practice and repetition to get your mind to associate the unique action stimulus with the memory you chose. But once you have put in the hard work, you can use it for your advantage by bringing to the surface all the empowering characteristics and feelings you had in your chosen memory at any time of your choosing. This might be before doing an interview or giving presentations or speeches and it can dramatically improve performance.

Sometimes, the so-called memory that you call upon as an anchor could be an imagined memory if it is powerful enough. It might be, for example, the dream of winning a gold medal or of climbing a great mountain. In his book Riding the Magic Carpet, Tom Anderson describes how having been brought up in South Wales, he dreamt of riding the right hand point break at Jeffrey's Bay in South Africa. He'd been inspired in the early 1990s when the combination of the release of Nelson Mandela, the ending of apartheid and the best surfer in the world was simply too much. The images of Tom Curren taking his first ride at Jeffrey's Bay were forever etched in the author's mind and the open face of the wave was associated with the ending of tyranny, with freedom itself. From this moment on he determined that he was going to ride that same wave. At a young age he created such powerful associations between Jeffrey's Bay and the concepts of freedom and perfection that they were so strongly anchored as to spur him on an odyssey which would take him all over the world as he prepared for the day he would arrive at Jeffrey's Bay. Many years later, he brought himself to the source of that abiding image and paddled out at his chosen wave where his dreams were rewarded.

Inspirations: Kate Winslet
Kate Elizabeth Winslet, born in 1975, is a BAFTA-winning and multiple Oscar-nominated English actress. She is noted for playing a wide range of diverse characters over her career, but is probably best-known for her role in the highest-grossing film of all time, Titanic (1997). The media, particularly in England, have enthusiastically documented her weight fluctuations over the years. She has been unusually outspoken about her refusal to lose weight in order to conform to the Hollywood ideal. She is known to keep magazines with pictures of unhealthy body images out of her house, in case they are seen by her 6-year-old daughter, Mia.

Quotations from Kate Winslet

It's so disturbing, because young girls are impressionable from 11 up to 19 or 20, even. Women are very impressionable at those ages...They're trying to figure out who they are, and they want to be loved, and what I resent is that there is an image of perfection that is getting thinner and thinner, and it's truly upsetting to me.

I hope that in some small way I'm able to say 'I'm a normal person, I'm doing all right, I've got a lovely husband and children and I didn't lose weight to find those things, and those things are what should be important.'

PART II

COMMUNICATIONS

Dear God, be good to me,
The sea is so large and our boat is so small.

A Breton Fisherman's Prayer

Communication is about listening to the messages we are given and responding with our own messages. It is one of the most valuable resources available to any professional and is the key to harnessing your most valuable resource, people. Effective communication builds rapport and ultimately relationships between individuals. It can also be used in the art of persuasion. Whilst obviously very different, the way the surfer communicates with the ocean can to some extent help to highlight some of the skills we all need. Above all, it highlights the most important part of communication which many people often forget: listening.

This section on communication analyses some of the key elements in building relationships, from the building of rapport and body language to more general skills of advocacy. The key thing to remember is that charm, charisma or eloquence which appear to be innate to some can to a large extent be broken down into their constituent parts and with practice be acquired. Once this has been achieved, these skills will help you not only in your professional life but also in your day to day living where such skills are equally as valuable.

Whilst some of the techniques may seem contrived and potentially even insincere, they are not put forward in that context. Hopefully they will help everybody to understand more fully how they communicate and to improve the effectiveness of that communication. Sincerity depends upon your own intentions after that.

Chapter 7

RAPPORT

there is nothing more enticing, disenchanting, and enslaving than the life at sea.

Joseph Conrad, *Lord Jim*

Introduction

Just as any surfer or sailor has truly to get to know the sea if they are going to spend any time there, so it is with human interaction, particularly if you want to persuade people to your cause. Abraham Lincoln once said, "If you would win a man to your cause, first convince him that you are his sincere friend." The building of relationships both with clients and with one's fellow workers is absolutely essential to any business. Clients will tend to return to those with whom they have enjoyed working. Indeed, research has demonstrated that 83% of all sales are based upon the customer liking the sales person. So, too, with employees who have been shown to be more apt to stay in jobs where they feel liked and appreciated.

While this may all seem obvious, the question that arises is why some people appear to find it easier to get on with people than others. Whilst no doubt it comes naturally to some, many others have had to work hard on their ability to build relationships. This ranges from the ability to chit chat with anyone to gaining a deeper rapport with others and ultimately to an ability to persuade and lead others. In this respect, this chapter will examine some of the building blocks in this process and in particular will look at some of the constituent elements of the building up of a rapport with someone.

The biggest part of gaining rapport is to take an interest in that other person. Surfers again show us the way. When they are surfing at their local spot they know every nuance of the bay at every stage of the tide and therefore feel at one with the waves. However, when they visit a new spot they have to use all their skills to get to grips with it. These include asking questions from the locals, watching how the waves work out different conditions and examining every detail of the coastal scenery which might give them a clue as to how the waves might work. Only surfers who like a spot will want to get to know it properly. Only those who do so will enjoy it into the long term. So it is with human relationships.

Rapport generally
Think back to a time when you singularly failed in trying to convince someone of something you wanted. Now think back to a time when you succeeded in such a task. Compare the two situations. One of the most likely factors is that the for the person you managed to persuade you will have built up a certain amount of rapport by the time the decision was made and for the person who did not agree with you any rapport there may have been will probably have broken down.

We can recognise rapport when it is there and note when it is not. One of the biggest connecting factors when there is rapport is the finding of similarities. This can be physical in terms of mirroring each other's body language. It can be verbal in terms of tone and pitch of the voice and also in terms of the language used. It can also be emotional in terms of finding deeper common ground through shared experiences or values.

It shouldn't be forgotten that rapport can be built collectively and not only one on one. One of the greatest communicators of our own time, Bill Clinton, is a master in the art of building immediate rapport. This is not only when he is meeting and greeting but is best elicited when he is in front of a crowd. At that stage due to the vast differences in the individuals in an audience, many people fail to gain any rapport since they cannot see the collective personality and movement of the crowd.

What Bill Clinton successfully manages to do is immediately to show the crowd that he understands them through his facial features and body language but he then manages to take them from this initial feeling of rapport and to lead them to deeper levels of connection throughout the speech. In his caricature, Primary Colours, Joe Klein vividly describes the President literally feeling the collective pain of his audience through both verbal and non-verbal rapport building skills.

Listening
Bill Clinton's is a good example of the building of rapport through empathy, the ability to feel how someone else is feeling. The single most important factor in this respect and probably in building rapport generally is the ability to listen. People always warm to people who are interested in them. In addition, by listening you will also learn exactly what makes that person tick.

As part of listening, it is often helpful to ask people about their lives outside of work, for example what are their interests and whether they have any children. Remember the answers and follow these up the next time you speak. Also, look for things in common with the other person. Remember that sometimes the pleasure of a shared hobby or passion can be increased by not mentioning it immediately but holding back with some things on first meeting.

Look after the other person
If the setting is informal, check that the other person is comfortable and has everything they want. Ask them how they are feeling. Imagine that they have had a hard day and you are the hundredth person to walk in with a problem. Also, perhaps emphasise your attention on that person with the use of the word "you", for example, "You will love this", "Could you…" etc. Compliments are of course an obvious way of making people feel comfortable but come with the warning that they should not be

over-used or used insincerely. Instead, have an attitude of looking for the positive in someone.

Small talk

Small talk has an important function of settling people and building rapport before the real talking begins. Common topics are recent news events and one's own plans so be ready for such matters before they arise. However, remember that not all issues which are raised are necessarily going to be helpful to you. When you don't want to answer something, ask "Why would you ask that?"

Mirroring

One of the biggest elements of rapport is looking for similarities and common ground. Therefore, a useful strategy in building up rapport is initially to mirror or match what the other person is doing or saying and to in effect copy many of the characteristics and vocabulary which are apparent. This is in effect to fall into sync with that person. After this, it is then possible to start to lead that other person and to see them follow. This highlights the communication which is being made by people on a level other than the content of their conversations. In this regard whilst the figures vary, it is worth considering that studies on communications have shown findings along the following lines:

1. 60% of the message is conveyed by body language and visual appearance generally.
2. 30% of the message is conveyed by tone of voice.
3. Only 10% of the message comes through the words used.

With this in mind, we shall start with body language. However, before doing so it should be said that all of these techniques come with a warning that if they do not come across naturally to the other person but instead seem forced then they could actually do more harm than good. Practice is therefore recommended before putting them to use. Further, although much of this may seem contrived it is in no way meant to detract from the sincerity of your communication. Instead, it provides tools by which your ability to communicate and to listen can be enhanced.

Body language

When people are in rapport their body language tends to align themselves together. This is easily illustrated simply by a look in at any pub of an evening. As people warm to each other and start to get along, either building or re-building their relationship they naturally align with people's posture and movement. Body language is a fascinating subject and for a more detailed examination, a good starting point is Allan Pease's Body Language.

Exercise

> When you are out with someone you know well on an informal occasion try mirroring your friend's body language in every respect. Cross your legs when they do, put your hand in the same place, copy the facial expressions and movements of the head. Notice the congruence and rapport which builds.

> When you have mastered this, take it a step further and once you have gained physical rapport, try leading your friend with certain movements and gestures. You will find that if you have gained enough rapport that person will then start to follow your lead.

> Then turn it around and try mis-matching your body language with that of your friend, in other words take on different gestures and movements. Notice the feeling of incongruence and breakdown of rapport in consequence.

Use of space

So, too, people align themselves in their use of space. For example, friends very often will sit next to each other or at right angles and share the space available. On the other hand, business meetings are often conducted face to face which in isolation can potentially be confrontational and certainly a matter of defining one's own boundaries. This can be used in management. When a manager wants to assert authority she can have people sit across the desk. When she wants to build up rapport or deepen a relationship, she can share the space and put the seats at right angles to each other.

Voice patterns

The same applies to the voice in terms of tone, pitch and pace. Rapport can be built by mirroring the features of the voice of the person you are talking to. When you have gained enough rapport you can then start to lead them into the type of exchange you are seeking. For example, somebody might start talking to you in a high pitched voice and at great speed from which it is easy to tell that this person is stressed and not open to having to take on new tasks or ideas. However, if you first mirror their voice patterns and then start to lead you will find that you will be able to slow down the pace and also potentially to make the tone of the delivery lower. In doing this you will be able to calm them and open them up to the possibility of accepting a suggestion and at the same time be gaining a rapport which you will then be able to use when finally making your request.

Vocabulary and figures of speech

Another way in which rapport can be built up is through a process called echoing which is basically looking out for particular words or figures of speech which the other person might be using and then either to take on those and use them back or to run with similar ones. This can be particularly useful with clients in showing them that you recognise their worries by articulating those worries in their own language.   An example might be if you were trying to communicate a difficult message with someone who loves surfing. In those circumstances metaphors such as "paddling running against the current", "riding the wave", "going with the flow", or "getting wiped out" may help to facilitate the communication.

Visualisation

One way of increasing rapport is to do a short visualisation before you go into a meeting. Close your eyes and imagine that the person you are going to meet (whether you in fact like them or not) is an old friend or customer for whom you have deep affection. Think of reasons why you would have this affection and the past (fictional) history you have shared. When you finally enter the room you will be far better prepared for your meeting than otherwise.

Telephone manner

When you have to talk on the telephone remember that most of the above points continue to apply. Don't treat it as a completely different medium. For example, the body language that you hold when talking on the phone can often come through. It's sometimes useful to try smiling before answering, to hold your head high and to remember to sound cheerful even if you're not feeling particularly happy at having to answer the phone. Remember also when you telephone somebody that you are entering their own private space. Check that it's a good time. If the person you are ringing has a secretary or a spouse who usually answers for them, make friends with them too. Courtesy and good manners can take you a long way.

Producing long term rapport

However good your skills in building rapport become the only secret to building long term rapport is sincerity and competence. However, the skills set out above will help to develop a trusting environment from which you will be able to build.

Inspirations: Mohandas Gandhi

Mohandas Karamchand Gandhi (1869 – 1948), was born in Porbandar, and went onto study law at University College London. He was called to the bar of England and Wales by Inner Temple, but had limited success establishing a law practice. He went onto become a major political and spiritual leader of India and the Indian independence movement. In India, he is recognized as the Father of the Nation.

Gandhi first employed his ideas of peaceful civil disobedience in the Indian community's struggle for civil rights in South Africa. Upon his return to India, he organized poor farmers and laborers to protest against oppressive taxation and widespread discrimination. Assuming leadership of the Indian National Congress, Gandhi led nationwide campaigns for the alleviation of poverty, for the liberation of women, for brotherhood amongst differing religions and ethnicities, for an end to caste discrimination, and for the economic self-sufficiency of the nation. Throughout his life, Gandhi remained committed to non-violence and truth even in the most extreme situations.

Gandhi dedicated his life to the wider purpose of discovering truth. He tried to achieve this by learning from his own mistakes.

Quotations from Gandhi

When I despair, I remember that all through history the way of truth and love has always won. There have been tyrants and murderers and for a time they seem invincible, but in the end, they always fall — think of it, always.

An eye for an eye makes the whole world blind.

There are many causes that I am prepared to die for but no causes that I am prepared to kill for.

Chapter 8

ADVOCACY:
PREPARATION AND TACTICS

And the voices in the waves are always whispering to Florence,
in their ceaseless murmuring, of love - of love, eternal and
illimitable, not bounded by the confines of this world, or by
the end of time, but ranging still, beyond the sea, beyond the
sky, to the invisible country far away!
Charles Dickens, *Dombey and Son*

Introduction

The beauty of nature and its wild gifts touches the soul of anyone who paddles out into the surf. It can take that person to another dimension. To a deeper knowledge both of himself and perhaps of something greater. However grand it might sound, the great advocate also has the ability to inspire us in such a way. To bring out the very best in ourselves. It is something which is often forgotten in this context. It is not just about winning arguments, persuading, cajoling. It is about something far greater. A clear communication from one person's mind to another. Whilst the detailed constituents of a great advocate may sometimes seem functional and even mundane, the bigger picture should not be forgotten. Do as surfers do when they are sitting out the back waiting for the swell to roll in. Look to the horizon. Know your place in the natural world and harness the forces around you.

As for general advocacy, it comes in all shapes and sizes. From the closing speech to a jury, to arguing your point in the office or even simply a domestic dispute, they all involve the same thing: the art of persuasion. As with rapport, it's often thought that this is something which either comes naturally or is impossible to master. However, in recent years this has very much been shown not to be the case as the teaching of advocacy has developed enormously. This chapter deals with preparation and tactics and the next chapter deals with the words and pictures which may be used.

Listening

Possibly the most important and also the most under-rated of all advocacy skills is that of listening. The most important details are gathered not from great oratory but by picking up on what either the judge or the person with whom you are debating with is saying. Judge's can give crucial indications that often go unnoticed. Witnesses too, can very often mention something merely as an aside which could change the whole complexion of the case. When you are listening to someone face to face, it's worth taking an active part to show the speaker that you are taking in what they are saying. Nodding, responding and maintaining appropriate eye contact can all help. The danger in not listening carefully to what is being said is illustrated by the following somewhat apocryphal transcript of which there are a number of different versions, this one being between a US navy ship and a Canadian authority:

U.S. Navy: Please divert your course 15 degrees to the north to avoid a collision.

Canadians: Recommend you divert *your* course 15 degrees to the north to avoid a collision.

U.S. Navy: This is the captain of a U.S. Navy ship. I say again, divert your course.

Canadians: No. I say again, you divert *your* course.

U.S. Navy: This is the aircraft carrier USS Lincoln, the second largest ship in the United States' Atlantic fleet. We are accompanied by three destroyers, three cruisers and numerous support vessels. I demand that you change your course 15 degrees north, or counter-measures will be undertaken to ensure the safety of this ship.

Canadians: This is a lighthouse. Your call.

Preparation
Next to listening, the other secret of advocacy was once correctly described as "preparation, preparation, preparation". In preparing whatever it is you want to argue, it is worth following a particular structure each time. The first thing to do is ask the so-called "5 Ws": what, why, where, when, who – in other words to elucidate all the details of exactly what you want to argue. Once you've done this, the techniques of mind-mapping and then boiling your arguments down to three key points really help to clarify what you are doing.

Mind-mapping
One technique for organising your thoughts is that of mind-mapping. This is far less complicated than it sounds. In effect it involves drawing a box in the middle of a piece of paper with the name of the problem within it. From that draw lines outwards for each of the main points or sub-boxes. From those, other points will follow and so on. When it is finished you will have a graphic representation of the problem on a sheet of paper. This will help more easily to organise your thoughts and also to remember the key issues when you start to argue.

Three main points
When you have completed your mind map, boil your argument down to a maximum of three main points and write them down. When arguing, it is imperative to stick to these main points and avoid the arguments becoming too general. It is very common when conducting an argument that people stray from the point and onto other territory which has been bothering them. Leave these issues for another day. They will only serve to undermine the points you do need to make.

If you are making a speech then once you have your three points you can add around that an introduction and also possibly a peroration or summary of what had gone before, artistically emphasising the favourable points and undermining those of the other side. However, these should flow naturally from the three main points you have chosen. Avoid simply reading from a written speech if you can help it.

Self-confidence

People often have a fear of speaking in public. However, they forget that they are perfectly capable of making speeches, something most people do in conversations with their friends.

Reading aloud

One way to try and overcome the fear of simply opening one's mouth to an audience is to practice in groups with a set piece such as a poem or an extract from a play. Alternatively, exercises can be done whereby people speak for just a short time about something they are passionate about or even what they did, for example, last summer.

Mind's eye exercise

You may also want to do the mind's eye exercise for overcoming fears, which was mentioned in chapter 3. This would involve playing the internal movie in your head of you speaking in public. Switch up the lights, play it backwards and forwards and play silly music over the top of it. Feel how the fear subsides as you see it in a different context.

A new identity

Another way to increase confidence is to visualise that you are in a different role before going into the argument or speech. You could imagine, for example, that you are an old experienced barrister, you could be *Rumpole of the Bailey*, you could be any empowering character you choose. When visualising, imagine you are walking into the argument as that other person taking on all their characteristics and appearance.

Your perfect state

Perhaps the most effective visualisation of all is to take yourself back to a time when you felt truly at one with the world, where everything was going well for you. Imagine where you were. Look first at this image in the third person. Then look at it out of your own eyes from that time, in other words in the first person. Then switch up the volume and the light and feel exactly how it felt at that moment. Notice the changes that take place in your own physiology when you stop the visualisation and try and keep as many of those changes as possible.

Preparing for your audience

Psychology
A major part of preparing is to make sure that you know and fully take account of your audience. This is inherently related to listening carefully. A particular approach with one person might have quite the opposite effect on another. Not only is it important to take account of everything you may know about that person professionally but also anything else you might know. As Lord Macmillan said in his *Law and Other Things* in relation to addressing a judge: "The judicial mind is subject to the laws of psychology like any other mind. When a judge assumes the ermine he does not divest himself of humanity..."

Put yourself in the other's shoes
It is also important to anticipate the sorts of arguments which will be put against you. One way of preparing for a speech or argument is to spend a few minutes beforehand visualising you are the person you are going to persuade or to argue against. Imagine in particular what it feels like to have to listen to the arguments you want to put. Not only will this help to gain rapport as mentioned in the last chapter but also it will help you properly to prepare for the arguments you are going to face against you.

Negative or positive motivations
A particular psychological distinction that is worth bearing in mind is looking at people's underlying motives. In this regard, some people generally do things in order to avoid something negative. Others do them in order to gain something positive. For example, someone might want to take up projects which will make profits whereas another might only look for things which do not make a loss. Very often the decision may be the same but the means of reaching that decision can be coming from completely different directions. When arguing with someone it is enormously

advantageous to have elicited that strategy beforehand. One way in which this can be done is to ask the person what exactly they are looking for and the reasons for that. If the setting is more formal then you may have to be more sophisticated in picking up where that person is coming from, via the answers and comments given. Once you have found out what is driving that person to make decisions then you can formulate your arguments in that way. In the example given above, if the person is an avoider then you will emphasise elements of the project which are safe and go towards guaranteeing that at the very least no loss will be made.

Mars or Venus

Along similar lines, in *Men are from Mars, Women are from Venus*, John Gray describes a difference between men and women in the way they approach problems. He says that men's first reaction is to want to fix everything whereas women very often want to be understood and have the problem discussed before fixing it is even considered. The authors do not suggest that such generalisations are accurate but they may provide a distinction at least between two personality types and how they might approach problems.

Win without a struggle

In *Tao Te Ching, Lau-Tzu* said, "The best soldier does not attack. The superior fighter succeeds without violence." This applies equally to the art of persuasion. There are a number of aspects to this and most of all it means approaching the problem in a positive and constructive way, being flexible in your approach and potentially ready to compromise.

Aim for no losers

If you are in a dispute with someone it is important to approach it with them on the basis that there will be no loser. Whatever the outcome you will both come out ahead. This does not mean being weak. On the contrary, it actually means that the other side needs to see the long term effect of not compromising, for example, on their business relationships or the cost of a dispute compared to the gain from looking at the problem realistically now. You may well need to re-define either the dispute or the process in order to do this. The art of compromise is making wise choices in what to give up, the so-called one step back for two steps forward approach, or what the French call *reculer pur mieu sauter*. General S. Patton was well aware of the benefit of such a move when he said: "We're not retreating, we're just advancing in another direction".

Avoid disagreeing

This may seem an absurd suggestion in the context of an argument but one of the most effective strategies is to agree in principle with what is being said but to put a slightly different perspective or spin on it so that it goes in your favour. The advantages of such an approach were articulated by Benjamin Franklin, one of the authors of the American constitution, "When another asserted something that I thought an Error...I began by observing that in certain Cases or Circumstances his Opinion would be right, but that in the present case there appear'd or seem'd to me some Difference etc. I soon found the Advantage of this Change in my Manners."

An exercise which can be used to practise this technique is for yourself and a friend to invent a subject about which to argue but whilst your friend argues in his own way you do so explicitly without disagreeing about anything. Instead, you could say, for example, "I agree and there's another point..." or "That's a really good point which reminds me of..." or "I appreciate what you're saying. Have you thought about this..." In this context, be imaginative in re-framing the way people look at the problem. As Proust said, "The real voyage of discovery consists not in seeking new landscapes but in seeing with new eyes." An example is that it is said that when a mother pleaded with Napoleon for mercy for her condemned son, Napoleon replied, 'He does not deserve mercy,' whereupon the woman responded, 'But sire, would it be mercy if he deserved it?"

Criticise in a positive context

Since argument is inherently confrontational it is often to one person's advantage to take the sting out of it and in doing so to take some of the power. This can be done, for example, by only making criticisms in a positive context, for example of more general praise. If there are any criticisms which can validly be made against yourself or your case, take them on the chin and if necessary, apologise. This can reduce tension and increase the chance of compromise.

Be reasonable

It can also be done by conceding your bad points. These concessions are illusory since you are likely to lose on those points anyway. However, it may lead to more substantive concessions by the other side. It also has the side benefit of avoiding the watering down of your bad arguments. In addition, it is sometimes helpful to concede that the other side have an argument, albeit one with which you do not agree. In return, this may well lead to the other side recognising that you too have an argument which can bring down resistance to compromise of some sort. As part of the same approach, remember that people always give far more resistance if they feel they are being rushed or they are being forced to do something. Give them time to consider. Present options or choices. The skill is in making the one you want to seem the most attractive.

Role reversal

A mediation technique which can help bring the two people in dispute closer together is to have them play out a role reversal whereby they have to argue from the other side's perspective.

Interrupting the flow

Whilst trying to agree with the other side can help much of the time, if someone is getting carried away with a particular argument and getting more and more emotionally attached to it and against your own, it can be useful at that stage to interrupt this pattern. This could be through the use of a polite question accepting what the person is saying but asking them about another particular variation of that issue. Alternatively, it could be through doing or saying something completely out of context which distracts attention away from the argument and potentially lowers the temperature of the debate.

Delivery

As well as having to work out how to deal with your opponent or any judge, it is also important to be clear as to how you are going to put yourself across. A number of points arise.

Speech

One of the most common traits of the inexperienced advocate is speaking too quickly as a result of nerves. Erring on the slow side is certainly something which will help to make your message clearer. However, simply keeping the pace slow could end up sending your listener to sleep and so variation of pace is in fact the key. If you want to emphasise something you might slow right down to get the listener's attention. However, if you are perhaps coming to the end and wanting to up the energy levels then speeding up might also help. Vary the pace so that the listener continues to follow what you are saying. The same applies to tone and volume in terms of varying it and using it to bring extra effect to what you are saying.

Manners

Good manners (or as Sydney Smith once called them "the shadows of virtue"), humour and general likeability are all absolutely essential to the advocate. However, as with all these things don't go over the top so that it strays into the realm of affectation which will have the opposite to the desired effect.

Personalising

Sometimes, it adds power to an argument if you can in some way personalise it. If you are arguing on behalf of your own case then you may use the word "I" more than you normally would to add your own personal power to the argument. However, if you are arguing on behalf of someone else (for example, at court) then you may instead personalise it to your client. Emphasise the effect which any particular argument and issue has on that person and refer to them by name more often than you might usually do. However, be careful not to overplay this or to lose objectivity as a result.

Understatement

When making your arguments it is generally better to slightly understate rather than overstate your own arguments. As C.E.Montagu once colourfully described this as, "casting your bread on the waters, under the form of a kind of rebate, in sure and certain hope that it will return to you buttered."

Address your difficulties

Most of the time it is often important to address the difficulties in your own arguments before they are put without answer by the other person or side. Very often this can disarm your opponent by putting your own spin on their arguments before they've had a chance to start. However, be careful not to play up or take the other side's arguments too seriously on all occasions as otherwise it could backfire. A characteristic of most people when they see someone in trouble is what Lord Macmillan once called the "instinct of rescue". This can sometimes be used when you are having to address your own difficulties. Judges are always impressed by honesty and by putting your difficulties they may not only warm to you but also sometimes even jump to your rescue with the arguments which you were intending to put. It is always more powerful if the judge thinks of the answer himself rather than you having to provide it to him.

Body language

Body language is an important part of advocacy which should not be overlooked and people should be aware of the various messages they may unconsciously be sending. In particular, it is important to ensure the speaker's physiology is congruent with the message. Before breaking it down into constituent parts, probably the most important part of this is that the speaker must believe what he is saying. If this is the case, the body language will generally follow. A good example of physiological congruence was David Cameron's speech at the Tory Party conference in 2005. It was delivered with a clear belief that he had the ability to be the next opposition leader. He stepped onto the conference platform and moved towards the audience with the physiology of a political leader. On a more specific basis, there are a few basic bits of body language which you can watch out for.

Nervous gestures

Everyone has them, they are movements our bodies make when we are nervous. Many people do not realise they have gestures and it comes as a surprise when they see a recording of themselves. It may seem obvious but control the gestures that you make in any argument. They should be, if anything at all, limited and gentle. In particular avoid any nervous twitches or moving too much. It not only takes the attention away from what you are saying but it shows weakness in your own arguments.

Defensive

Defensive or closed positions should be avoided if at all possible save where it might be part of a mirroring exercise in order to lead straight afterwards. This includes crossing of the arms or legs.

Openness

The opposite of these gestures are more open ones suggesting that you are open to the ideas of the other person as well as indicating that you have nothing to hide. One of the most powerful ways that people indicate this is through the use of the open palms and wrists. An extreme example of this is the big speech to Congress by James Stewart in *Mr Smith Goes to Washington.*

Deceit and doubt

Other types of gesture to be avoided are those often associated (though obviously not always) with deceit or doubt. A classic gesture in this regard is that of the mouth guard. This is where the hand covers the mouth and the thumb is pressed against the cheek as the brain subconsciously instructs it to try and suppress the deceitful words that are being said. Sometimes this gesture may be only several fingers over the mouth or even a closed fist, but it's remaining can be the same. Many try to disguise this by giving a fake cough. This gesture was famously used by Humphrey Bogart when discussing criminal activities with other gangsters or being interviewed by the police to show non-verbally that he was being dishonest.

Evaluation
This gesture is not to be confused with evaluation gestures. These
are where a closed fist is rested against the cheek often with the
finger pointing upwards.

Boredom and criticism
Two things of which the advocate should be aware when such a
gesture is being made is when the evaluation process either moves
to boredom or where it indicates negative or critical thoughts.
Boredom is generally obvious to people and that is where the hand
moves from mere evaluation to the palm of the hand supporting
the head. Negative thoughts are indicated where as in evaluation
the hand is on the cheek and the index finger pointing upwards.
However, in this situation the chin is supported by the thumb.
Often also the index finger may pull or rub at the eye as the
negative thoughts continue. Once either boredom or criticism sets
in the best hope for the advocate is to try and interrupt that
particular train of thought. One way can be to involve the listener
in what he is saying or indeed even to end what he is saying.
However, another way is to do a simple move such as handing
something to the listener which will immediately change his
position.

Decision-making
A crucial time for any advocate is when the other person
approaches the making of a decision. The gesture most often
associated with this is that of stroking the chin. Either the advocate
can choose to interrupt the pattern or accept that this may be the
last chance saloon and get his best points in at that point.

Inspirations: Atticus Finch (famously played by Gregory Peck)
To Kill a Mockingbird, a 1960 novel by Harper Lee, is told from
the point of view of Jean Louise Finch, the six year old daughter of
Atticus Finch, a lawyer in Maycomb, Alabama, a fictional small
town in the Deep South of the United States. To the consternation
of Maycomb's racist white community, Atticus agrees to defend a
black man named Tom Robinson, who had been accused of rape.
He did so because of he felt a strong sense of morality to try and

save Tom from unfair prosecution. Through his decisions Atticus is a guiding light for his children, always being calm and patient. He teaches them that one should not dwell on the fact that evil exists, but that they should instead realize that the existence of this evil is a sign that there is work to do, and progress to make. Despite Atticus providing clear evidence that the accusers are lying, and significant evidence pointing to Tom's innocence, the all-white jury convicts him. The innocent Tom later tries to escape from prison and is shot to death.

Quotation from Atticus Finch

You never really understand a person until you consider things from his point of view... until you climb into his skin and walk around in it.

Quotations from Gregory Peck

I put everything I had into it – all my feelings and everything I'd learned in 46 years of living, about family life and fathers and children. And my feelings about racial justice and inequality and opportunity.

You have to dream, you have to have a vision, and you have to set a goal for yourself that might even scare you a little because sometimes that seems far beyond your reach. Then I think you have to develop a kind of resistance to rejection, and to the disappointments that are sure to come your way.

Chapter 9

ADVOCACY:
WORDS AND PICTURES

Here, throwing themselves upon their boards, tranquilly they wait for a billow that suits. Snatching them up, it hurries them landward, volume and speed both increasing, till it races along a watery wall, like the smooth, awful verge of Niagara.

Herman Melville, *Mardi*

Introduction

In chapter 4 we looked at how important words and pictures were to the running of the internal mind. So, they are equally important when communicating to someone else's mind. Words are important for lawyers from the contracts they pore over to the pleadings they write to the arguments they run in court. However, words have a far higher purpose and in considering any form of advocacy it is always worth remembering. Words are the bridge between peoples' minds. They are the means of communicating thoughts which otherwise might be trapped in the imagination. They are a means of bringing us together.

Roger Payne, one of the world's leading whale specialists and the man who recorded the whale songs which were sent out into open space in the *Voyager* mission understands the importance of words to human life. In *Among Whales*, he goes as far as to say that the story of *Moby Dick* conjured so powerful an image of the whale that it would "enter our minds, and...once inside...metastasize and diffuse throughout the whole engine of human ingenuity". Ultimately, he suggests that might even go so far as to re-connect us with nature so that we "make the transition from Save the Whales to Saved by the Whales."

Another image which has entered our minds and diffused throughout the engine of human ingenuity is that of surfing itself in relation to the internet. It provided a perfect description for the freedom and movement which the information superhighway could provide not only in the sharing of information but also in connecting communities together, just as the oceans flow from one to another. Some surf writers have railed at the idea that non-surfers should be acquiring this word and particularly for something which couldn't on the face of it be further from paddling out into the sea, perhaps most articulately by Andy Martin as far back as 1995. Writing in *The Independent*, he commented that, *"the sinister implication...is that 'There is nothing beyond the Web.' Being is being on the Net"*. He *suggested a compromise, "I promise not to lose my cool every time you surf the Net on the condition that if you slip and press the wrong key you download death in a million-volt wipeout."*

However, just as whales may ultimately save us by firing up visions of the natural world, so it is with surfing. Computer hacks the world over may be using the word without much thought but underneath they are stoking the fires of their imagination. It is the ocean in the human soul which is awakened by these gentle breezes. Our deeper selves. They have always been in us. Whales. Surfing. They are the routes within. The means.

Words

Be yourself

When making an argument it is always important to choose your words carefully. However, never lose sight of the human element of the communication. People very often over-formalise their speech when they start offering a formal argument whereas they would be much better served just saying it how it is. However, that is not to say that sometimes a single word cannot be decisive and you have to be aware not merely of the literal meaning but also of the references that that word may conjure up to the listener or reader.

Tell a story

When putting a point it's often helpful to tell a story which people are often much more likely to remember as opposed to a collection of random arguments. Always remember therefore to keep your narrative.

Accuracy

It is imperative that whatever argument you are putting you are accurate. Persuasion does not involve exaggerating your case as not only is that ethically wrong it will also serve to undermine your case in the long run.

Clarity

Simplicity and clarity are essential to good advocacy as they are taken to reflect the strength of the arguments. Good arguments, however complicated they may be, should not appear so if at all possible. You want to make it seem like you have the obvious solution to the problem and clarity only goes to serve this aim. Consider the power of the words of Winston Churchill in 1940, "We shall not flag nor fail. We shall go on to the end. We shall fight in France and on the seas and oceans; we shall fight with growing confidence and growing strength in the air. We shall defend our island whatever the cost may be; we shall fight on beaches, landing grounds, in fields, in streets and on the hills."

Concise

The length of a speech or argument depends upon the context but the general rule is that if in any doubt veer on the side of being concise rather than lengthy. Once again, it helps to persuade that your argument is the obvious one but it also keeps the person who is listening attentive. This is obviously not the case if it is clear that you are losing the argument and more work is needed. However, consider the power of the short phrase which was offered by President Kennedy in his Inaugural Address, "And so, my fellow

Americans, ask not what your country can do for you; ask what you can do for your country."

Choice of words
As was mentioned in the chapter on rapport, so it is with advocacy generally. If you know that your listener has a particular passion or interest then you could associate your argument with it by using metaphors or other figures of speech which evoke that particular thing. For example, if someone loved surfing, you could use a phrase like "riding the wave of success". For someone with a boat you could suggest "keeping the company afloat" or for someone who likes gardening "sowing the seeds".

Be measured
One of the most important things for the inexperienced advocate is to avoid going over the top. Perhaps having read too much *Rumpole of the Bailey* they approach even the simplest speech as if it's a closing speech in a murder trial. This will only serve to irritate the person listening.

Focus on the destination
When making a presentation or putting forward an argument, people can sometimes suffer from panic attacks halfway through. The important thing in these circumstances is not to focus on every detail of the here and now but instead to keep in the forefront of your mind the point your are trying to make, the direction you are taking. This is equally the same with surfing. In *West of Jesus*, Steven Kotler described the best advice he "had ever been given about surfing" as the following, "...don't look at the section of the wave that is about to slam closed on top of you, but look past it to the place where the wave's shoulder is, and usually you will end up there."

Metaphor
Whilst we have discussed the power of the metaphor on the internal mind, it is its effect on the outside world which can have the most far-reaching effect. Lawyers may conjure up an image, for example, of a feather balancing on the scales of justice or quote Shakespeare's "The quality of mercy is not strain'd, It droppeth as

the gentle rain from heaven". Politicians, too, have the use of metaphor as one of their primary tools. Consider the following:

> *I know I have but the body of a weak and feeble woman; but I have the heart of a king, and of a king of England, too. (Queen Elizabeth I)*

> *I have a dream that one day even the state of Mississippi, a state sweltering with the heat of injustice, sweltering with the heat of oppression, will be transformed into an oasis of freedom and justice. (Dr Martin Luther King)*

> *The nation had the lion's heart. I had the luck to give the roar. (Winston Churchill)*

Visual aids

Just as the use of the imagined image in the metaphor is useful, so is the physical image which can sometimes be used to facilitate an argument. In particular, it can help anchor an argument or point in people's minds. When using such visual aids it is also important to keep attention to the other person's gaze so that they associate what you are saying with what is being shown to them on the screen or board. To maintain maximum control of the listener's gaze, you could use something to point to the visual aid and at the same time verbalise what he sees. If you then lift the pointer and hold it between his eyes and your own eyes it has the effect of lifting his head so that he is looking at your eyes. He then sees and hears what you are saying which achieves maximum absorption of your message.

Silence

What should not be forgotten when reflecting on communication is that the words which are passed from one person to another are only a part of the whole picture. The moments of silence in between are also important. In *Voyage of the Turtle*, Carl Safina said, "Poet Laureate Billy Collins says poetry should displace silence, so that before the poem there is silence, and afterward again, silence again." The sea turtle's poetry, he said, was that it displaced water which afterward was still. Just as the surfboard also displaces the water on the surface of a wave, so our words displace the still moments which surround them. To appreciate this is to add yet another dimension to our understanding of how ultimately we relate to each other.

Inspirations: William Wilberforce

One of the greatest struggles for a better world, was the fight against slavery which waged for two hundred years. In England, at least, it was William Wilberforce (1759-1833) whose untiring devotion finally carried the day to what at times, seemed a hopeless cause. At the age of 21 he was elected an MP and after Wilberforce found religion he was soon looking for a cause to champion which could allow his passion for Christianity expand into social affairs. Happily, the group working for the 'Abolition of the Slave Trade', were at that moment seeking a leader who could carry their work on the floor of the House of Commons. Enormous interests opposed it; Bristol and Liverpool had practically been built on the profits of the infamous trade. British shipping had become enormously profitable by trafficking slaves from Africa to America; plus colonies in the West Indies depended upon it.

Wilberforce brought two great phases. The first, making the carrying of slaves on British ships illegal and the second, to free all slaves under the British flag. He faced a mammoth fight as even when he got laws passed despite enormous opposition in the Commons, they were defeated in the Lords. Abuses were blinked at; slaves were continued to be sold openly on the streets of Liverpool. However, Wilberforce never faltered during the 20 years it took to get the Bill against slave trade passed. In the final debate members of the house praised his untiring devotion which had made it all possible. His second Bill to abolish all slavery under the British flag took another 25 years of battle. Just two days before his death the House of Commons passed the final measure to abolish slavery. His life work was crowned with glory, eight thousand slaves became free and the stain was washed from the British flag.

Quotation from William Wilberforce

True Christian benevolence contracts itself to the measure of the smallest, expands itself to the amplitude of the largest.

Chapter 10

THE POWER OF QUESTIONS

The sea is everything. It covers seven tenths of the terrestrial globe. Its breath is pure and healthy. It is an immense desert, where man is never lonely, for he feels life stirring on all sides.
Jules Verne, *20,000 Leagues Under the Sea*

Introduction

E.E.Cummings said, "Always the beautiful answer who asks a more beautiful question." So, it is both in law and in life. Surfers may ask questions such as "where do the winds come from?" and "where do they go?" They certainly ask such day to day questions such as. "what direction is the wind?" and "what time is it high tide?" Whatever it is they ask, questions are the route by which they get to the answers.

As for lawyers, questions are as much the tool for them as advocacy itself, indeed probably more so. Asking the right questions is crucial from the moment a client walks through the door to the day the case arrives at court and the other side's witnesses need to be cross-examined. However, the skill of asking the right questions which is acquired through practice can also be applied to both the rest of our professional lives as well as to personal development. This chapter will take a brief look at the way questions are used in practice and it will then look at how these skills can be applied elsewhere.

Case preparation questions

The difference between a well-prepared case and one that is not is very often the failure to ask the right questions. When a client approaches a lawyer with a legal problem he does not know which of the multitude of facts in his possession are the relevant ones. Only through thorough questioning can the full information be elicited. It may sound trite but if over-looked it can lead to at the very least embarrassment and at worst an action in negligence.

In the asking of questions, lawyers need to be wary of answers which are based upon assumptions. The assumption upon which it is founded may end up being inaccurate or even untrue and eventually undermining the whole case. Something which is mentioned as just an aside to a very small question can lead to a whole new avenue of enquiry. It's therefore always worth having the following question in mind when preparing a case: "Is it possible that I have missed anything, however, small, in questioning the client."

Courtroom questions

Witnesses
When it comes to court and you're examining a witness on your own side then the general rule is that leading questions are not allowed. This means that you have to become versed both in asking very general open questions and then being able to direct a witness' attention without suggesting the answer. Cross-examination is quite the opposite and is filled with leading questions. Indeed, some say that you should use nothing else.

Types of questions
In *The Technique of Advocacy*, John Munkman designated names to the various types of questioning used in cross-examination. These are particularly instructive due to the wider use to which they can be put. They are:

    a.   *Probing questions* which are designed to elicit information to tie the witness down to a particular account of events. These are particularly helpful when a witness may have given a different account on an earlier occasion and you are therefore building up to a later confrontation.

b. *Insinuating questions* which can be used either to get the witness to make damaging admissions and also to put your case to him.

c. *Confrontational questions* which mean literally confronting the witness with something and where very often the element of surprise can help.

Repetition and ridicule

In eliciting the information sometimes it might be effective to repeat a question if it has not properly been answered the first time. A classic example of this was the Newsnight Interview of Rt Hon Michael Howard MP by Jeremy Paxman. However, it should be used sparingly, particularly in civil cases. Generally, a judge will have got the point the first time. Ridicule can also sometimes be an effective tactic in discrediting a witness. However, if a witness has said something which is blatantly absurd, the understatement is generally the most effective way of casting ridicule. Sometimes simply getting that person to confirm what they have said is enough.

Have a theory

When cross-examining a witness it is generally important to have a theory as to how something happened to put to that witness. Remember also to consider asking about events leading up to and those following a particular event. The more material and events there are to ask about the more chance you have of catching someone out. However, the major caveat to this is the classic advice of avoiding the question too far. Once you have got what you want from a witness be careful about going any further. That final clarification could potentially undermine the points you have already scored.

Expert witnesses

When cross-examining expert witnesses, a slightly different approach has to be taken. The first is to look at the possibility of discrediting that witness, for example, through his qualifications, background or conclusions. The other approach is to try and establish an alternative interpretation of the facts upon which the expert's opinion is based.

The suggestibility of witnesses

The type of questions which are asked in court leads onto the question as to how witnesses respond to questions. In particular, the extent to which witnesses are susceptible to suggestion from leading questions. The Devlin Committee was established in 1973 and looked at over 2,000 legal cases in England and Wales involving identity parades. It found there was overwhelming weight given to eye-witness testimonies and went onto recommend that trial judges be required to instruct the jury that it isn't safe to convict on a single eye-witness testimony. This recommendation is underlined by a famous case of misidentification involving an Australian psychologist. The psychologist in question had appeared in a TV discussion and was later picked out in an identity parade by a very distraught woman who claimed that he'd raped her. The rape had in fact occurred while the victim was watching the psychologist on TV. She correctly recognised his face but not the circumstances. This is source confusion or as psychologists would say *source misattribution.*

According to Fiske and Taylor (1991), it's also easy to see how a witness could confuse the mention of something in a question with its actual presence at the scene of the crime, if that something is commonly found in such situations. Others argue evidence given by witnesses in court cases can be unreliable, especially if leading questions are asked which might confuse. Lawyers are skilled in asking such questions, but is it possible witnesses may be misled into remembering things that didn't actually occur?

The effect of changing a single word in questions has been tested by psychologists (Loftus and Palmer). In one example participants were shown a 30 second videotape of 2 cars colliding, then they were asked questions about the collision. Some participants were asked "About how fast were the cars going when they hit?' For other people the word 'hit' was replaced by 'smashed', 'collided', 'bumped' or 'contacted'. These words have very different connotations regarding both the speed and force of impact, and this was reflected in the estimated speeds given.

People who heard 'smashed' gave a speed estimate of 40.8 miles per hour (mph), people who heard 'collided' gave an estimate of 39.3 mph, people who heard 'bumped' gave an estimate of 38.1 mph, people who heard 'hit' gave an estimate of 34.0 mph and people who heard 'contacted' gave an estimate of 31.8 mph. The significance between 'smashed' and 'contacted' gave a change in the estimated speed of 9mph. In other words, witnesses are potentially highly suggestible.

The witness statement, true or false?
After asking questions to witnesses, lawyers are also considered to be generally good at spotting deception. However, research would suggest that the success rate of spotting deception is lower than the rate of determining deception by just tossing a coin. Indeed studies show that people can detect lies in others at a rate of only 44%. Even professionals who are meant to have a lot of specific experience in this area, like police officers and customs officials, perform no better at lie detection than at the level of chance.

It matters crucially for many professions, including lawyers, to spot deception. In one famous experiment police officers were exposed to videotapes of people who were asking the general public for help in finding their missing relatives. Some of these people had already been found guilty of crimes against their relatives, but police officers were unaware of this. What was found was that none of them performed any better at spotting deceit at the press conference than could be expected by chance. The psychologist Professor Aldert Vrij, who conducted the experiment, found that the only professionals more adept at spotting deception than the general public were officers who worked for the US Secret Service; but then again they tended to trust no one at all.

One explanation as to why professionals are no better at detecting lies than the general public is that they are burdened with the same false beliefs about how liars behave. For example, it is commonly preconceived that liars have key non-verbal behaviours, such as gaze aversion. However, the opposite may hold sway because liars have to manufacture reality, and this usually requires a lot more intellectual effort than simply reporting the truth. As well as watching their words, liars tend to monitor closely how their story is coming over hence, liars tend to concentrate on the listeners more intensely instead of looking away. Therefore, perhaps someone who maintains more eye contact than usual is the person to be concerned about. Also good liars tend to make fewer gestures to try and ensure that they don't 'leak' body language clues.

It is said that a useful tip is that liars experience three main emotions during lying: fear of being caught, excitement at the opportunity of fooling someone ('duping delight') and guilt. By being vigilant for these emotions, it is supposedly possible to spot them in facial movements that appear for short time periods of time and betray these emotions. Unfortunately these expressions are usually barely perceptible to most intense concentration, but they may be helpful tips under the scrutiny of the court room.

Negotiation and meditation
The skills set out above which lawyers use in court can also be applied to other areas. The most obvious is in dealing with other types of dispute which are not court-based. A technique which can be used in negotiation is to ask your opponent questions about their own case and about their views on your own case. In this respect, questions can be used to put a completely different perspective on an issue. If you are at loggerheads with someone and then you ask them how you can both win from this situation, it changes the whole way of looking at the problem. Rather than looking at trying to win on every little point you both start addressing the issue from the direction of compromise.

Another situation where questions can very often be the key is in a mediation. Indeed, one of the mediator's key tools is the asking of the right questions in order to get people to change their approach to the problem. As well as asking how the two parties might both benefit from the situation, another question which can be used to try and interrupt a heated confrontation is to ask the two parties to address the question of what is good about the situation they are in. This completely changes the focus. For example, the very fact of having had a dispute may be seen as a positive in that ironically it could bring the parties closer together in the long run.

Questions for business
The skills we use with clients can also be used when dealing with our own business situations more generally. Those which are listed below are merely illustrative of the types of questions which can be helpful. Remember when entering upon such an exercise bear in mind the skills set out above which can be transferred from the arena of, for example, the court room into other areas of your life.

Business problem questions
Questions can be the key to unlocking the problems which any business is facing. Again, they can help change the focus from the here and now and in particular the negative cycle which a problem can cause. This is particularly so if the business is experiencing difficulties. These can be used by lawyers both for their own business and potentially also for their clients. The following questions could then be of help in changing the focus away from the negative effects of a particular problem:

1. *What is good about the problem we are experiencing?*
2. *What has this problem taught us?*
3. *How can we avoid experiencing this problem in the future?*
4. *How can we use this problem to help us in our future development?*

Business development questions
Business development is dealt with in Chapter 15 and one of the key strategies in planning for the future is to ask the right questions. As well as asking the general empowering questions set out above, it can be followed with more specific questions about enhancing the business for the future. Examples of such questions might include:

1.   *How can we add more value to our existing clients?*
2.   *How can we increase our number of clients?*
3.   *How can we enhance our reputation further?*
4.   *How can we work more efficiently?*

Questions for personal development

In chapter 4, we saw how questions can be used to help to turn a problem around in one's mind and to take a fresh and positive approach to it. Such questions can also be used more generally in personal development. For example, although they might seem a little cheesy or earnest, answering the following questions can often help to empower.

1. *What is great about my life?*
2. *What value do I add to people's lives both at work and play?*
3. *What people have I helped in my life and in what way?*
4. *Who are the people who love and support me?*

The same also applies to prioritising and looking to the future. The very act of asking the questions gets the mind moving towards answers whether it is always conscious or not. Examples might be:

1. *What is most important to me in my life?*
2. *What do I want to achieve in my personal and professional lives?*
3. *How can I move towards those goals?*
4. *How can I help people more in my personal and professional lives?*

Inspirations: Lois Gibbs

Lois Marie Gibbs, (1952) is an environmental activist whose involvement in environmental causes began in 1978, when she discovered that her 7-year-old son's elementary school in Niagara Falls, New York was built on a toxic waste dump. Subsequent investigation revealed that her entire neighbourhood had been built on top of that same dump, the Love Canal.

With no prior experience in community activism, Gibbs organized her neighbours and formed the Love Canal Homeowners Association. She led her community in a battle against the local, state, and federal governments. After years of struggle, 833 families were eventually evacuated, and cleanup of Love Canal began. National press coverage made Lois Gibbs a household name.

The words 'Love Canal' have been burned into history as being synonymous with chemical exposures and their adverse human health effects. The citizens of Love Canal provided an example of how a blue-collar community, with few resources, can win against great odds (a multi-billion-dollar international corporation and an unresponsive government), using the power of the people in democratic system.

Quotation from Lois Gibbs:

In 1978, my neighbours and I discovered that our neighbourhood in Love Canal, New York, had been built next to 21,800 tons of buried toxic chemicals. When we bought our homes, none of us knew that...We [just] knew there were too many miscarriages, too many birth defects, too many central nervous system problems, too many urinary tract disorders, and too much asthma and other respiratory problems among us.

PART III

TAKING ACTION

O Lord God, when Thou givest to Thy servants to endeavour any great matter, grant us to know that it is not the beginning, but the continuing of the same unto the end, until it be thoroughly finished, which yieldeth the true glory: through him who for the finishing of Thy work laid down His life, Our Redeemer Jesus Christ. Amen

Sir Francis Drake Prayer

Once you have decided to do something, the thing which will distinguish you from the crowd is the very fact that you follow up this good intention with action. Very often this may mean breaking away from the crowd. Geothe said of boldness that it has "genius, power and magic in it" and it is true to say that those who break the mould, who lead the way, have the ability to inspire others.

When Roger Bannister broke the elusive four minute mile in 1954, it was only another six weeks before someone else followed in his footsteps and many more were to follow within a short time. So, too, when Hillary and Tenzing summated Everest in 1953, they would probably never have imagined the number of people which were to follow them in the decades to come. Of the world's most challenging wave, the Banzai Pipeline, Sam Moses described the first ride which was made by Phil Edwards in 1961, "The Pipeline went untouched for years. After Edwards surfed it, he looked over his shoulder and saw three of his buddies paddling toward the lineup."

Of course, taking action doesn't mean that you have to do something extreme. Nor is it merely about worldly things which are recognised by others. As T.S.Eliot said, "The awful daring of a moment's surrender / Which an age of prudence can never retract / By this, and this only, we have existed". It can be the very smallest things which make all the differences in our lives and changes to these can change our whole directions.

In this section therefore, before we look at goal setting, time management and business development, we therefore look at how we can take action in the more private realm of emotions and identity. However, whether they are to do with how you feel or what you are doing, the most important thing of all is that you take action now. Stop procrastinating. Don't wait for tomorrow. As Mark Twain said, "Twenty years from now you will be more disappointed by the things that you didn't do than by the ones you did do. So throw off the bowlines. Sail away from the safe harbor. Catch the trade winds in your sails. Explore. Dream. Discover."

Chapter 11

EMOTIONS

Give us back our suffering, we cry to Heaven in our hearts—
suffering rather than indifferentism...out of suffering may
come the cure...A hundred struggle and drown in the breakers.
One discovers the new world. But rather, ten times rather, die
in the surf, heralding the way to that new world, than stand
idly on the shore!

Florence Nightingale

Introduction

Einstein pointed to the fact that waves are manifest in all areas of
our physical world. We see through the medium of light waves and
hear through sound waves. Waves transmitting bundles of energy.
So, too, with surfing. Farber in *On Water*, "These children at play,
singing the song of the sea." Jack London pointed out that the
water itself does not move forward. It is only energy and "The
water that composes the body of a wave is stationary. Thus, you
may watch a particular portion of the ocean's surface and you will
see the same water rise and fall a thousand times to the agitation
communicated by a thousand successive waves."

Billy Hamilton, one of the great surfers of the 1960s and step-
father of big wave surfer Laird Hamilton said, "To become the
energy of the waves, that's the main idea. You take when the water
gives, and you give when the water takes". In *Voice of the Wave*
(re-printed in *The Surfer's Journal*), Tom Blake, one of the
founders of modern surfing went further and suggested looking
inside the wave itself and further still to the secrets it holds at an

atomic level. He said, "Each water molecule...is a model of order, harmony and rhythm; thus the atom becomes the key point of reference...in judging the wave as well as all problems in life." So it is with looking to our emotions. They are like waves, the steady heartbeat of our soul. They are subtle, complex and not altogether clear, much like the constituent parts of a wave. They are fundamental to our very existence.

Listening to emotions

When a big wave looms on the horizon the following might occur: increased heartbeat and blood pressure, dryness of mouth, sweating, dilation of the blood vessels, increased production of adrenaline and release of glucose. These changes are an efficient response to the perceived threat of the wave and help our bodies to respond appropriately either by paddling for it or escaping from it. In this way, emotions can be extremely useful in triggering physiological responses which can help us through life. Whilst this is an extreme example, what it illustrates is that it is important to listen to our emotions as they are often good indicators of what is going on around and within ourselves.

The one caveat to this is that sometimes the body can trigger the feeling of particular emotions based upon false evidence, in other words, the system can break down. For example, if someone accidentally falls from their surfboard in a relatively calm sea, they may be thrown somewhat for a while and feel fear where there is in fact no need. Whilst we have to be aware that this can happen, it does not diminish the importance of listening to their gentle whispers.

Emotions and their meanings

By asking what the emotion and feeling might mean, you are taking the first step towards listening to the messages of your soul and ultimately to controlling those emotions. The following offer a few examples of emotions that might elicit negative feelings but which in fact could be giving you very positive messages. The suggestions are generalisations only.

Frustration

Frustration may mean that your brain believes you could be doing better than you actually are which can be a very constructive way of feeling. The goal is still in reach and the message may well be simply to look for other strategies of attaining it. However, it may also mean that you have to try and be a little more patient. In *Gift from the Sea*, Anne Morrow Lindbergh said, "Patience, patience, patience, is what the sea teaches. Patience and faith. One should lie empty, open, choiceless as a beach — waiting for a gift from the sea."

Disappointment

Disappointment on the other hand may well suggest that the goal is now unobtainable and the message in those circumstances might be to change goals rather than merely strategy.

Overwhelming

Feeling overwhelmed may mean that be that you need to re-evaluate and prioritise. The first step in re-routing this emotion is to gain a sense of control over what's going on. Sometimes, writing down a list down and putting them in order of priority can be helpful. Then tackle one thing at a time on the list and continue to take action until you've mastered it. As soon as this ordering is done, your brain will have gained some momentum and hopefully feel less overwhelmed.

Guilt

The feeling of guilt may sometimes be telling you that you have broken one of your own standards. The pain can be used to help you try to avoid doing this again in the future.

Stress

Stress can be used to drive you in the direction you desire and can be channelled to generate energy, utilized as a useful tool rather than a treated as a foe. However, the feeling of stress develops when there is mismatch between what you think you can do and what's expected of you (including expected by yourself). The message is that you need to take stock and evaluate this mismatch.

Society can often exacerbate this situation with extra pressure. Consider the example of the 'superwoman syndrome' where women of today sometimes seem to be expected to do everything. They may be expected to be the main carers for the husband, children, parents and friends, to be successful in business and to keep the house. All whilst recycling the waste, being fashionable, fitting energy saving light bulbs and every other societal expectation. Do you think this is expecting too much? Even Cherie Blair, mother of four children, top barrister and wife to a world leader was forced to tackle this expectation syndrome and knocked it on the head by saying "I am not superwoman." Men, too, can feel the pressure of expectations. Perhaps expecting to be strong, sensitive, successful, wealthy, good cooks and emotionally supportive. Role models should not be cartoon characters and we all need to beware of these pressures and how they impact on our well being.

Dealing with stress
Challenge can have very important effects on the brain and its neurotransmitters. Noradrenalin is a key chemical messenger in the brain, like our very own 'wake-up' drug. However, it can also be linked to stress and severe stress can lead to hyper-vigilance. When this happens it can be very difficult to concentrate on anything. When stress is at a moderate level it can sometimes be invigorating and motivating. But beware as severe stress and prolonged stress can have negative effects on the brain.

A recent survey commissioned by the Samaritans confirmed that Britain was one of the most stressed nations in Europe. It showed that twenty percent of Britons felt 'their life was out of control'. The following provides a few general suggestions and tools for dealing with stress:

- Take time out from stress. This this will prevent unhealthy obsessing.
- Get a good night's sleep.
- Never be afraid to ask for help or advice. The chances are someone else will have faced a similar task.

- Think what you would advise someone else in the same situation. We are often good at solving other people's problems, so why not use your own advice?
- Confide in someone. Remember the old saying 'a problem shared is a problem halved'.
- Stop beating your self up. Everyone makes mistakes.
- Avoid imagining that the problem is worse than it actually is.
- Divide tasks into chunks. Take each source of stress in turn and think of three ways of increasing your control, even if this is to a very tiny extent.

The final point about gaining control of the stressful situation is perhaps highlighted by a famous psychology stress study, in which participants were asked to work on a task that demanded a lot of concentration. The task was made even more difficult by adding a level of background distraction noise whilst the participants were trying to complete the task. This noise addition induced a stressed feeling in the volunteers. Volunteers were then told that they could switch off the background noise if they wanted to, by pressing a button. Their stress levels immediately dropped, simply knowing that they could push the button if they wanted to, even though they hardly ever did. This shows that stress may partly be due to the work demands made on you, but it's also due to the stress you put on yourself. When you gain a sense of control or even potential control over this, it can be a great stress antidote. Hence, taking even small steps to increase your control over a stressful task, can really help reduce the overall stress level.

Exercise: how to exert control over stress
Think about the sources of stress in your life. For every area of your life when you experience stress it is very likely that there is something you can do to reduce it. It doesn't matter how tiny the step you take, or how small the reduction in stress it brings about, exerting some control – any control – can help break the vicious cycle of helplessness and inaction. Whether the stress is related to

work, family, health, money or anything else, even writing a priority list may help order the mind and exert the first step in control.

Inspirations: John Muir

John Muir (1838-1914) was born in Scotland and attended the local school of a small coastal town, where he developed his love of the natural world. He became one of the earliest modern preservationists via his direct activism to help try and save the Yosemite Valley and other wilderness areas. But more than that he helped to change the way we look at the natural world by considering the value of nature for its own sake rather than just practical value.

His free time was occupied by his pursuit of science, especially geology, and he taught the people the importance of experiencing and protecting our natural heritage. His words have heightened our perception of nature. His personal and determined involvement in the great conservation questions of the day was and remains an inspiration for environmental activists everywhere.

Quotations from John Muir

Climb the mountains and get their good tidings. Nature's peace will flow into you as sunshine flows into trees. The winds will blow their own freshness into you, and the storms their energy, while cares will drop off like autumn leaves.

Keep close to Nature's heart... and break clear away, once in awhile, and climb a mountain or spend a week in the woods. Wash your spirit clean.

So extraordinary is Nature with her choicest treasures, spending plant beauty as she spends sunshine, pouring it forth into land and sea, garden and desert. And so the beauty of lilies falls on angels and men, bears and squirrels, wolves and sheep, birds and bees....

Chapter 12

SELF ESTEEM

In the old days...My friends and I would sleep in our cars and the smell of the off shore wind would often wake us. And each morning we knew this would be a special day.

Surf movie, *Big Wednesday*

Introduction

Let's take a moment to identify who you are. Identity can have many facets. It can arise from one's activities. Even the fact you are a lawyer, gives you a certain identity. Surfers often find identity in surfing too. Some people on the other hand find identity in emotions, such as being 'highly strung' or 'laid back'. Others identify themselves with possessions, such as a 'Porsche owner'. Others with religious beliefs. Sometimes people take on a single identity almost to the exclusion of all else. In *Stealing the Wave*, Andy Martin describes how big wave surfer Ken Bradshaw came out of Texas and took on the North Shore of Hawaii. For him surfing was not just something which he happened to be doing. It defined him. Just as Michelangelo took a block of marble and might produce an elephant by carving away everything that did not resemble such an animal so it was for Ken Bradshaw and surfing. Everything else was jettisoned. However, most people's identities are a mixture of many different facets.

Whilst this is always evolving, its importance lies in whether our actions are consistent with our internal view of ourselves, our identity. The difference between self-identity and the way we act, can cause tension, and even set the stage sometimes for an identity crisis. An example of conflict between inner and outer congruency was seen in John Melius' surf film *Big Wednesday*. It highlights what for many surfers is a conflict; the fight between so-called soul surfing and commercialisation. In the film, the protagonist Matt Johnson is seen to rail at the increasing commercialisation of surfing. In the meantime, his childhood mentor Bear has set up a surf shop to cater for the mass market. Despite the fact that Matt is falling apart, he is still portrayed as the romantic hero defending the old values of surfing, refusing to sell his soul. When Bear offers him a board to endorse, he replies: "I just surf because it's good to go out and ride with your friends." Later, exasperated, he cries, "You oughta know what I mean, Bear!" This also illustrates that congruency is specific to each individual. Whilst the above example would appeal to some surfers' view of themselves and of surfing, others would see no conflict at all, pointing out that commercialisation means for example, better wetsuits and board design.

The importance of identity
Does self-identity itself make any difference? In 1973 the 'Prison Simulation Experiment' gave a real insight into how the brain manages an identity. Male participants were recruited through newspaper advertisements, asking for student volunteers for a two-week study. Twenty-four suitable and healthy participants were selected. They were then randomly assigned to their role in this prison experiment, as either 'prisoner' or 'guard' and a mock prison was set up. On the first morning, those allocated to be prisoners were unexpectedly arrested by local police and charged with felony, read their rights, searched, handcuffed, fingerprinted and taken to the basement prison. Upon arrival, prisoners were stripped naked, searched, deloused and issued with prisoner uniforms and bedding. Prisoners were referred to by number only. The guards wore uniforms, reflective sunglasses (making eye contact with them impossible) and carried whistles, clubs, handcuffs and the keys to the cells and main gate. Guards were on duty twenty-four hours per day, working eight hour shifts. They had complete control over the prisoners, who were kept in their cells, except for meals, toilet privileges, head counts and work.

After an initial rebellion had been quashed, the prisoners began to act passively and the guards stepped up their aggression each day. For example, guards had a head count in the middle of the night simply to disrupt the prisoners' sleep. After less than 36 hours one of the prisoners had to be released because of uncontrollable crying, fits of rage, disorganised thinking and psychological depression. Three others developed similar symptoms and another developed an all over body rash after his 'parole' request was rejected. The whole experiment, which was planned to run for two weeks, was abandoned after just six days due to the prisoner reactions. One of the guards later said "I was surprised at myself – I made them call each other names and clean the toilets out with their bare hands". Zimbardo et al concluded that the study showed the power of identity, and the power of social and institutional forces can even make good men engage in evil deeds. In other words, identity is flexible and can be changed by societal and other external factors.

Identity exercise

Bearing in mind the importance of identity, it is worth spending a bit of time exploring your own identity. Thinks about what Howard Martin said, "Don't ask the what the world needs – ask what makes you come alive and then go and do that. Because what the world needs is people who have come alive."

Then do the following exercise:

> *List all the elements you identify yourself with.*
>
> *Then think about who you would like to be.*
>
> *Then list the words you'd like to identify yourself with.*
>
> *Then commit to moving towards this identity in your actions.*

The Hierarchy of Needs

Maslow said, 'A musician must make music, an artist must paint, a poet must write, if he is to be ultimately at peace with himself. What a man can be, he must be.' Maslow himself distinguished between motives shared by humans and non-humans, and developed an increasing hierarchy where only humans are capable of reaching the top. He developed what he called the 'hierarchy of needs' based on the premise that individuals require satisfaction on an ascending level of need. He suggested that only after one level of satisfaction has been achieved, can the next level of need become important. It is a bit like climbing stairs with each level being a step. Maslow's famous steps are the following:

> Step 1: Physiological – this is the most basic level. It includes air, water, food, sleep and everything that is required for life compatibility.

> Step 2: Security – this encapsulates all that is required to be safe from harm, such as the need for clothing, shelter, personal safety and also includes fear of the unknown.

> Step 3: Social – this includes having people to talk to; people who will share thoughts and concerns. It's about developing family, friends and a social network with whom social bonds can form and become part of a team.

> Step 4: Self-esteem – this is about personal individual status; within our group each person has an individual status and role that gives an identity.

> Step 5: Self-actualisation - this is about feeling satisfied with the given position and status; knowing that we have done the very best with all the talents and gifts we have. Realising one's full potential and 'becoming everything one is capable of becoming'.

The higher up the hierarchy you attain, the more difficult it can become to achieve the next level of satisfaction. The striving for goals in themselves is something which is arguably unique to human beings. The longer term the goal, sometimes the harder it is to pursue. Now ask yourself, how far have you travelled up Maslow's stairs?

Self-esteem

The distorted mirror

Starting at the fourth level, self-esteem. A large quantity of people suffer with low self-esteem, which is the fourth level. This can be caused by a bias in two complementary ways of thinking. First, a bias in perception and second, a bias in interpretation. Hans Christian Anderson wrote a story 'The Snow Queen'. At the beginning of the story, the devil makes a mirror. No-one who looks in the mirror sees a reflection of his or her true self, but instead they see a distorted image, twisted and ugly. Low self-esteem can distort self-perception in a similar way to the devil's mirror. It can distort interpretation, so rather than seeing a true reflection, what jumps out are specific self dislikes or perceived weaknesses and faults, yet inevitably differences make us all human.

Control the inner prosecutor

Perhaps poignantly for lawyers, in 1983 Burka and Yuen provided a clever way of describing how self-esteem tends to focus on the bad and ignore the good. They suggested that people who are down on themselves have an extremely vigilant, powerful and effective 'inner prosecutor', who is alert for every flaw and weakness and ready to condemn at the drop of a hat. Therefore what is needed is an equally strong 'inner protector', who will present the evidence for the defence. And then, finally and most importantly an 'inner judge' must be developed who, like a real judge, will take all the evidence into account and come to a fair and balanced view, rather than condemning solely on the evidence presented by the prosecution.

Therefore, low self-esteem can be combated by correcting biases and developing a fair inner judge and helping develop the 'inner protector'. The 'inner protector' may ask questions such as the following:

> *What do you like about yourself?*

> This can include anything, even fleeting thoughts or achievements.

What are your positive qualities, and what aspects of yourself would you appreciate if they were aspects of another person?

These do not necessarily have to be measurable qualities, but could be things you may appreciate in others, such as kindness, honesty, punctuality.

Do you expect yourself to be perfect?

This is a common symptom of people with low self-esteem. It is reinforced by the 'never good enough' syndrome, which is simply not realistic, and opens the flood-gates to self-criticism, depression and feelings of inadequacy. It is impossible to get everything right one hundred per cent of the time, and by expecting yourself to do so is setting yourself up for failure. Accepting that you cannot be perfect does not mean giving up attempting to do things well, but is about setting realistic targets and praising yourself when you reach them.

Generosity

Helping others can automatically create positive self-esteem. Even things as small as helping an elderly person cross the road can have an affect.

Competitiveness

Another aspect of low self-esteem can be the making of comparisons with others. Sometimes, competitiveness itself may be a mask for low self-esteem. Life cannot always be compared. Instead of concentrating on what others have done, recognize your own achievements.

Self- Esteem exercise

Positive self-esteem empowers you to meet life's challenges and to consider yourself worthy of happiness. Focusing on your positive traits will immediately improve your chances of creating the life you desire and deserve and stop you from putting yourself down if this is something to which you are prone.

Take a moment to consider your past successes and achievements, both recent and further in the past. Make a list of twenty positive things you have done. These certainly do not have to be major achievements. It could even include something such as getting a piece of work in on time.

Think of at least ten positive qualities of which you are proud.

Ask five people you know well, to write down your top five perceived strengths and to give praise to the person you are.

Self-actualisation

Maslow's step five, self-actualisation is when all needs have been taken care of. It's the finding of what is most important to the inner self and expressing it. This is often the stage when people want to give something back to the world, on recognition that it has supported them in their journey of achievement up through the hierarchy. Others consider it a stage for the letting go of material desires and allowing themselves to live their life in congruence with their soul. However it is manifested, it can bring a sense of purpose, integration, maturity, health, and self-fulfillment.

Inspirations: Samuel Plimsoll

Upon the side of ships you should find the 'Plimsoll mark': a circle with a horizontal line across it to guarantee that no ship is loaded so heavily that the line is submerged under water. The symbol spelled life instead of death for untold thousands of sea merchants. It seems incredulous that ships were sent out to sea which were overloaded and not seaworthy, but were heavily insured. The men who sailed in these 'coffin ships' were doomed, no trade unions were there to defend them; no laws gave them any protection. Samuel Plimsoll, who was born in (1824, - 1898) devoted his life to championing their cause and fought for change via the House of Commons.

He published a book called *Our Seamen* which was an attack on ship owners, for the existence of the extreme evil of coffin boats and for the absence of humane conditions of life at sea. After much political debate, his book rallied the moral force of public opinion and the Merchant Shipping Act was passed, which empowered sea vessels to be examined and detained if deemed unsafe.

Quotation from Samuel Plimsoll

> *I cannot trust myself to say what I think or feel in plain English. I shall therefore put my feeling into my work. And, oh! How I will work!*

Chapter 13

GOAL SETTING

I have seen [the mermaids] riding seaward on the waves
Combing the white hair of the waves blown back.
                    T.S.Eliot, *Love Song of J.Alfred Prufrock*

Introduction
Unlike most sports, there is no scientific criteria for distinguishing success for a surfer. Every surfer knows what it is but it's often hard to put into words. In fact even to try to do so can potentially devalue it. Maybe it's catching the longest ride, maybe it's just getting out there and clearing your head of the day's chores. Maybe it's simply getting "stoked". Whatever it is, it's entirely subjective and the measurement for each person can even change from day to day. Surfing in this respect is more of an art than merely a sport. It is a means of self-expression. Of becoming something more and inspiring something deeper than merely the physical act.

With this in mind, it's pretty impossible for surfers to set down an objective set of goals which they can daily work towards. Sure, they might want to improve their bottom turn or cut back. But ultimately what it boils down to for each surfer is whether they feel that sense of stoke by the end of the session. They therefore approach it with a completely flexible agenda, looking to make the best of every time they paddle out, not quite knowing what is going to happen.

Rather than being defined by goals, surfers are defined by commitment. Commitment to life in all its glory, to riding nature's forces. Commitment to paddling out in all weathers, through all waves. Surfers learn pretty quickly that to suffer from 'rubber arms' where you simply go through the motions without actually getting anywhere is unsustainable. Commitment to paddling hard into waves that can truly terrify. One of the skills which a surfer learns early on is that if you're going to catch a wave you have to commit. The crucial moment comes just when it feels like you might not make it and you're looking down at a sizeable drop. The need to make that extra paddle, to jump up and to take the drop. In doing so, you almost join with the sea, become a part of it. Lord Byron described it in this way, "And I have loved thee, Ocean! ...I wanton'd with thy breakers...And trusted to thy billows far and near, / And laid my hand upon thy mane -- as I do here."

This also provides a very powerful metaphor for life itself. Many motivational books often get pre-occupied with the act of goal setting and in the process perhaps lose some of the soul, forgetting what it is really about. The goals are merely a means to a deeper end. This is not to say that goal-setting is not a powerful tool. Simply that it must be seen in context and if the path towards those goals is not quite straight then this must be seen as part of the great adventure rather than a deviation from the course. Goals can be good but they can also put a straight-jacket on creativity. They should be seen as setting a direction for the journey rather than determining the end of the journey in advance. When this is set, the key is to take action and commit with all the heart of a surfer paddling for a wave. The following should be seen in this context.

Effective goal-setting
The Latin derivation of the word 'motivation' means 'to move', hence the 'study of motivation' is the 'study of action'. There are many theories about motivation, yet there's no comprehensive way of examining it, no mathematical formulae for it and every person has a different motivation, as unique as their personality. At its heart, though is personal change and action. In order to make any change, you have to be specific about what it will take and what

needs to be done. Statements such as 'work harder' or 'you must do better' are not motivational in themselves as 'they are far too general. To facilitate effective goal-setting, the following commonly used acronym SMART can be very useful:

S - specific

M - measurable

A - agreed

R - realistic

T – time bound

To illustrate this by way of example, we can take the issue of weight loss, using the framework 'Be SMART to be kind', offers helpful motivational tips for weight loss:.

Specific
When setting a goal, be as specific as possible, don't be vague. If you want to loose weight you must consider the details of the weight loss programme such as diet, exercise, organisation etc.

Measurable
To be motivated to lose weight you need to know how much you weigh now, how much weight you want to lose and over what time period. Only by collating this information will there be a quantifiable scale to measure. This will help you to understand how to adjust performance in order to attain the set targets. Interestingly, tracking is unpopular as a motivational strategy, because it often involves receiving unpleasant feedback about how badly you are doing. However, unless you track then you have no idea how you are progressing, meaning you can not modify your behaviour to become successful.

Agreed
It is helpful to have an agreed and structured weight loss programme. Agree it by telling everyone about your plan to lose weight, as this makes it much less likely you will back out and also gives others the chance to offer support and encouragement. Involve others in your routine, this may include going to weekly gym classes with your friend. Link up with others with similar aims of weight loss so that you can all learn form each other.

Realistic
What is often overlooked as an important part of the strategy is that any plan must consider the resources necessary to attain the goals. For losing weight this may include a budget for buying scales, healthy food, gym membership, trainers and tracksuits etc. Also be prepared that there will inevitably be setbacks during the weight loss programme, but the key is not to let failure put you off persisting. Learn from failure. See setbacks as a resource and a learning opportunity, a necessary part of any journey. Be aware of your own weaknesses, since if you are aware of them you can think of strategies to overcome them. So, if for example, you know you have a weakness for chocolate midnight feasts, then you may decide upon a strategy of not keeping any chocolate in the house.

Time bound
Goals need to have a timescales for success. Sub-goals can be included within that timetable. Timescales adds pressure to help continuation with the vision. Tracking progress is an essential step in goal attainment but it's vital that you can be flexible as any completely rigid timetable is unlikely to work especially if goals are totally unrealistic. Plans may need to be revaluated, but don't get put off, keep up with the programme.

Finally, be kind to yourself, give yourself a break
Always remember to congratulate yourself on each success, this should be done throughout the programme with lavish praise each time your sub-goal target has been achieved. This will help you continue with the next target. Just as you plant a seed, you cannot force its development. However, you can provide the right conditions and environment for it to develop and grow into a flourishing plant. So it is with providing yourself with praise as you strive to succeed.

Goal-setting exercise
Once you have realised how to set effective goals, the next step is to brainstorm a few goal-setting lists. You might try these for both your personal life and your work life. Whilst remembering that these should not straight-jacket your actions in the future, it remains an extremely useful exercise to brain-storm over goals for a while. Try this exercise for starters.

Make two headings of personal life and work life and then write five things under each which you would like to happen in the short term (i.e. the next year). Then write down five things under each that you would like to happen in the long term (i.e. the next few decades). Next to each of these then write down five things which you will need to do in order to reach that goal.

This exercise is merely an example of how goal-setting can be used. It can be far more specific. For example, a firm might want to increase its profits. If this is the case, then you have started with the goal and you can immediately move on to how this can be achieved. In each of the goal-setting scenarios, remember to ensure that what you write lives up to the SMART criteria set out above.

Inspirations: Oseola McCarty

Oseola McCarty, (1908 - 1999) was born in Mississippi and as a young girl she dreamed of becoming a nurse. However, family duty stood as an obstacle to occupational goals, as when her aunt and grandmother became ill, she was forced to leave school to care for them. To make money she would wash and iron other people's clothes. Throughout her frugal life, she never married or had children and did not own a car. However, through saving she became The University of Southern Mississippi's most famous benefactor, and drew global attention after it was announced she had established a trust through which, at her death, an estimated $150,000 of her life's savings would be left for the philanthropic cause, to provide scholarships for deserving students in need of financial assistance.

In 1998, she was awarded an honorary degree and received other honors recognizing her unselfish spirit. President Bill Clinton presented her with a Presidential Citizens Medal, the nation's second highest civilian award. She also won the United Nations' coveted Avicenna Medal for educational commitment.

Quotations from Oseola McCarty:

I want to help somebody's child go to college...I just want it to go to someone who will appreciate it and learn.

I can't do everything, but I can do something to help somebody. And what I can do I will do.

Chapter 14

TIME MANAGEMENT

Time is but the stream I go a-fishin in.

Henry David Thoreau

Introduction

Time. Hours, minutes, seconds. Notes which are the measure of life and facilitate an historical perspective. Help us plan for the future. Yet there are some moments in our lives when we feel outside of time. Rising above it. Stepping outside of time's heavy march. Moments which engrave the soul; moments imprinted upon the memory before re-joining that march. Some surfers might say that this is how it feels when they are on a wave. Others might feel this in communion with God or in the purest moments of love or feeling at one with nature. It is the moments when the demands of time are forgotten that are often the most significant. Auden in *The Waters*: "With time in tempest everywhere...The waters long to hear our questions put / Which would release their longed-for answer, but."

Blake spoke about being outside of time, "[i]f the doors of perception were to be cleansed, everything would appear as it is, infinite." Yet time is used by everyone as a measure or a gauge. T.S.Eliot said that he had "measured his life out in coffee spoons". Most use the calendar, the seasons, the years and ultimately the generations. It helps to give meaning, perspective. Yet, if too much attention is given to the passing of time, perhaps the vision and the bigger picture is lost. If this is the case, it is certainly true for lawyers as they take the measuring of time to its extreme. They make it into a commodity. Something to be bought and sold. The amount of billable hours worked is translated into someone's worth to a firm.

This in itself can be no bad thing as it makes us all aware of the need to value the passing of time. Economists would describe time is a scarce resource and that any use of it has an opportunity cost, in other words they are stating the obvious: that you could have been doing something else instead. The risk for lawyers is that they always see this opportunity cost as a billable hour. This of course risks skewing the view of time, particularly when the price of perhaps the most precious activities can never be valued; as the Barclaycard ad says, are priceless. What price, the soul?

This Chapter is written with all of this in mind and examines not only how to organise time but also how to regard it in our professional and personal lives. Much of it is about being organised. Once again, this may be a good general guide but should be taken in the tone which it is given; everything in moderation. There is a place for organisation and there is also a place for its' opposite. As A.A.Milne said, "[o]ne of the advantages of being disorderly is that one is constantly making exciting discoveries."

Prioritise effectively
In organising time, be aware of Parkinson's Law which states:

> *Work extends so as the fill the time available for its completion...there need be little or no relationship between the work to be done and the size of the staff to which it may be assigned.*

It is extremely easy to prevaricate about a particularly difficult task which needs doing. However, the longer it is put off, the more stressful it can become. One useful way of helping to organise your time is to consider the table below.

Time prioritising exercise

URGENT & IMPORTANT	URGENT & UNIMPORTANT
NOT URGENT & IMPORTANT	NOT URGENT & UNIMPORTANT

Go through your 'to do' list and put each task into one of the four boxes. This will help you to focus on what tasks need doing and in which order. Obviously, the top priorities are those in the box marked "urgent and important". On the other hand, it can sometimes be helpful simply to cross off all those tasks marked "not urgent and not important". Bear in mind the words of Goethe, who said, "[t]hings which matter most must never be at the mercy of things which matter least." Therefore, try and distinguish and then de-clutter the tasks which are truly unimportant.

The most important box of all is that containing the tasks marked "not urgent and important". These are the ones which will cause long term stress if their number builds up. Hence, why not set yourself a goal of completing at least one of these tasks each week so that over time their number decreases. If you don't do this, they will slowly go from being "not urgent" to "urgent" and risk causing overwhelm if you are not careful.

Lists
Some people find it helpful to draw up 'to do' lists for the day and for the week and certainly these can help to focus the mind not only on what is to be done but also what has then been achieved at the end of each day. It may facilitate focusing the mind on priorities. However, if you are going to draw up such a list, don't put all the tasks together so that the inconsequential ones take on the same significance as the important ones. Go through a similar

exercise to that above and make a list setting out which are the most important things to get completed.

Invest time for the future
One of the key "not urgent and important" things for any business is that of business development. In fact, the time set aside to plan for the future is some of the most valuable spent by any business. However, a difficulty for those who bill out by the hour, such as lawyers, is that this type of work is intangible and does not have a value which can be assessed in the same way. It's therefore important that when making plans, time is explicitly put aside for this.

One way of bringing this into the culture of a law firm is to break down the distinction between billable and non-billable time. In this respect, the time spent on business development could be recorded in much the same way as billable time. It could then be taken into account as part of overall performance. This may also be reinforced through progress reports on business development ideas so that people can then see tangible results from their efforts.

Remember 80/20
A useful concept to bear in mind when organising your time is the so-called 80/20 or 'Pareto principle' which states that for many phenomena 80% of the consequences stem from 20% of the causes. In time management, sometimes it can be seen that around 80% of the work is done by 20% of the time spent. This is the most valuable and productive work and should be recognised as such.

Learning to say "no"
One of the most important principles in time management is avoiding over-commitment. In order to do this, it's important to learn the value of saying "no" to requests to do certain things. It might seem the easy way out at the time to say "yes" to something and therefore avoid disappointment. However, in the long run, it may cause far more aggravation and stress if it leads to over-commitment as not only will you risk letting people down but you will also put yourself under undue stress.

Delegation

Some of the most able people are the least capable of delegating. This is probably because they hold such high standards that they are unable to pass a task on for fear that it will not be completed as well. However, time is finite and failing to delegate carries with it the cost of not being able to take part in another opportunity. If you are one of these people it may be helpful to work on trying to let go. Ironically, rather than giving you less control, it can instead increase the area of your influence. However, as a word of warning on delegation, try and ensure that you do so effectively with very clear instructions and boundaries as to the tasks to be undertaken.

Finish what you started

One of the most effective ways of working more efficiently is to endeavour to finish what you started. It is very easy to get distracted and to move onto something which although less important, at that point in time, perhaps seems far more interesting. Remember the prayer of Sir Francis Drake, "O Lord God, When thou givest to thy servants to endeavour any great matter, grant us to know that it is not the beginning, but the continuing of the same unto the end, until it be thoroughly finished which yieldeth the true glory: through him who for the finishing of thy work laid down his life, Our Redeemer, Jesus Christ. Amen."

Planning for eventualities

Many people approach life on the basis that if a problem comes along, they will deal with it. Others seem to spend all their time worrying about what might go wrong and forgetting to live for the moment. Obviously, it's about getting a balance between these two extremes. However, the importance of being prepared for things going wrong should not be underestimated as it is something which can give you the edge over the competition. Given that lawyers are continually advising clients about making provision, for the unlikely event that something may go wrong, they should have a particular aptitude at making such contingency plans.

Work-life balance

Just as it's important to value non-billable time at work, it's even more important to value time away from work. This should always be absolutely integral to any time management plan and should not be seen as a bonus for when the other jobs are finished. Time should always be available for any partner, family and friends as well as your spiritual life more generally. This can be particularly difficult when things at work get busy, and this highlights the need to plan ahead. Don't just aim for time on holiday and weekends which are important. Try and put some time aside each day.

A Round Tuit
The late Dr Roger Morris of Magdalene College in Cambridge provided the Round Tuit below. If you find it of help, then perhaps copy it and pass it on to someone else.

A Round Tuit

At long last we have a sufficient quantity for each of you to have your own! Guard it with your life. These tuits have been very hard to come by, especially the round ones. This is an indispensible item. It will enable you to become a much more efficient worker. For years we have heard people say 'I'll do that as soon as I get a round tuit.' Now that you have a round tuit of your very own, many things that have been needing to be accomplished will get done.

Inspirations Wilma Rudolph

Wilma Glodean Rudolph (1940-1994) was born in Tennessee and was the 20th of 22 children, however, at early age it was discovered that she had polio. It took her until the age 12 until she could walk normally. Despite this she decided to become an athlete on the influence of a track coach. She lost many of her early races. Slowly she went from last, to second from last, to first in all her races.

When she was playing for the basketball team of her junior high school, she was spotted by the track and field coach. She went onto became a track star, competing at the 1956 Summer Olympics at the age of 16 she managed the outstanding achievement of winning a bronze medal in the 4x100 m relay. At the 1960 Summer Olympics in Rome she won three Olympic titles; in the 100 m, 200 m and the 4 x 100 m relay. It was her desire to use her personal triumphs to open doors and smooth paths for others, who like herself, started out with the odds against them.

Quotation from Wilma Rudolph

I would be very disappointed if I were only remembered as a runner because I feel that my contribution to the youth of America has far exceeded the women who was the Olympic champion.

Chapter 15

BUSINESS DEVELOPMENT

More majestic than the thunders of mighty waters,
more majestic than the waves of the sea,
majestic on high is the LORD!

Bible, Psalm 93

Introduction

In *Surfer's Code*, ex-surf world champion Shaun Tomson describes how he was the victim of surf rage back in the 1980s. Someone had pushed in front of him in the queue, what surfers call 'snaked him'. He took the wave anyway and pushed that other surfer back into the breaking part of the wave. Later on, he was punched on the beach by that same surfer. Twenty odd years later he reflected on this incident and on the issue of anger in the water in general which is becoming increasingly topical as surfing becomes more popular and the big breaks more crowded. In hindsight he accepted that although the other surfer was in the wrong, the whole incident could have been avoided if he had had in the forefront of his mind the principle that "there will always be another wave". In *Surfing and the Meaning of Life* by Ben Marcus, world surfing champion Kelly Slater is quoted as saying, "Next time someone takes a wave off you in the water, know there is probably a better one on the way...Sometimes the best gifts are hidden where you can't imagine they would be."

This is a point that it is easy to forget not just in surfing but in life in general. When an opportunity is missed for whatever reason, it may seem as if nothing like that will come along again. New opportunities will present themselves if you are looking just as surely as waves will continue to break on our shorelines.

This chapter will encourage the reader to look at business development in the wider perspective and hopeful. It will also give a few suggestions. Whilst these could not hope to be in any way comprehensive, it is hoped that some of them may prove either useful in themselves or inspiration for other developments.

Principles
Before looking at specifics, it's worth looking at a few general principles which might assist in one's approach to business and work in general.

Generosity
In the same vein that it is always important to remember that "there will always be another wave", it is also important to remember that business does not tend to be what economists call a 'zero sum game'. In other words in any particular market there is rarely, if ever, a limited pie which must be divided out between competitors. Instead, the whole system of capitalism is based upon the principle of wealth creation. Innovation, creation, production. Since the first tools were manufactured and bartered for food, human beings have advanced. The pie is therefore unusually capable of expanding. This is worth bearing in mind when considering whether or not to collaborate with a potential competitor.

Flexibility
In *Who Moved My Cheese*, Dr Spencer Johnson explains the importance of dealing with change at work and in one's life generally. Those that survive are those that anticipate change and therefore plan for it, going out and looking for new business and ways of doing business before the old source has dried up. Change, in this sense, should be treated as a constant. Something to be welcomed, a source of opportunity. Just as surfers need to keep their eyes to the horizon, watching the subtle movements of the ocean to judge what type of waves will be coming along, so it is with business.

Integrity

It is important not simply to focus on the spreadsheet and what the nearest competitors are doing. If you take a step back, it is crucial to remember that the foundation stone of business is that of adding value to people's lives. Of course, you need to get the right structure in place to make the profits follow. But without any adding of value, no structure or other form of alchemy will work.

This is part of a bigger principle, that of the importance of integrity to business. This is all the more so in the professional world of law. Although it might sound over the top, drafting a mission statement or a set of core principles for the business can provide a number of benefits. Not only do these act as positive influences on day to day decisions but they can also help to forge an identity which in its turn will help to inspire those within it. In addition, a mission statement written and executed with sincerity can only have a positive effect on client confidence.

The same can be said for the many forms of corporate and social responsibility programmes which businesses can now consider. These are excellent ways that businesses explicitly recognise the wider context in which they exist, both at a society and an environmental level. So, businesses may well support particular charities and also have specific policies on the environmental impact of their business. These can again help to provide a common set of values around which the whole firm might rally.

Patience

Patience is as important in business as it is in any other area of life. In the context of the sea, Anne Morrow Lindbergh said the following in *Gift from the Sea*, "The sea does not reward those who are too anxious, too greedy, or too impatient. To dig for treasures shows not only impatience and greed, but lack of faith."

Inspiration

To succeed in most businesses and work you will need to harness the power of other people and in order to do this it is important to remember the importance of inspiration. As Antoine de Saint-Exupery said, "If you want to build a ship, don't herd people together to collect wood and don't assign them tasks and work, but rather teach them to long for the endless immensity of the sea."

When you are concentrating on developing your relationships with existing clients as well as expanding your future client list, it should never be forgotten that a firm's human capital is the most important element of its business. Make sure that everyone is involved in the goal setting and business development process, however junior. Team building exercises always serve a useful purpose but firms should be aiming to invest in their people every day of the year. This can be through funding (non-compulsory) training courses to bringing in people to help people develop not only their professional but potentially also their personal goals.

Ambition
Just as it's important to set goals for yourself it's also important to set goals for your business, both short term and long term, something that is covered in Chapter 13. Make sure that these goals are not limited to your current perspective on the business but encompass the possibility of broadening its scope in some way if appropriate. Whether it is to start up a business or an extension of an existing business, entrepreneur Ben Finn, one of the founders of the music software company Sibelius, has emphasised that it can always be a useful exercise to write out a business plan. This will focus the minds of the main people in the business onto issues such as the main advantages of the product, the size and composition of the market, the competition, the pricing structure and plans for the future. It will also help overcome one of the biggest challenges facing many businesses which is maintaining perspective in the face of the day to day details.

Responsibility
The simple act of asking for feedback can in itself help to improve a relationship with a client even if that feedback is not necessarily positive as it means that you are directly taking responsibility for the service you provide. It will also help you to find out which parts of your practice and business you need to work harder on. Feedback can be sought both informally on the telephone or more

formally with a form. It can also be sought by a visit to the office of a valued client where the opportunity can be taken to discuss in more detail exactly what they are looking for and where you might not be delivering in quite the way they would hope.

Marketing

There are numerous books and guides to marketing and it is not intended here to provide a comprehensive guide. Instead, it will simply raise some of the types of marketing which might be applicable in the legal world. These are in addition to standard types of marketing such as the use of advertising, direct mailing etc..

Lectures and seminars

A valuable method of marketing to clients is through the giving of lectures and seminars. This type of marketing not only gives you access to clients and provides general goodwill but it also positively adds value to them by being informative and ultimately useful. There are numerous firms specialising in providing lectures and they are always looking for new speakers. In addition, your clients' trade associations and other such bodies may have events in which they need speakers. Alternatively, a firm could arrange its own seminar and invite a range of different clients. Pick on key areas of specialism within the firm which you want to play up and direct it at those. For particularly important clients, you might consider visiting their office and giving a more informal talk or perhaps a training seminar for their employees. Remember also that if the content is good enough these do not necessarily have to be free. Don't forget seminars can now be online and cut down on travelling time and carbon emissions. These are called 'webinars' (web seminars). For an example see the site of CPD Webinars (www.cpdwebinars.com).

Articles

Writing can an enormously effective way of marketing, perhaps the simplest form. Not only does it provide advertising, it also adds to the reputation of the writer and the firm. Aim at publications which are read by your clients and potential clients. A useful system would be to set up a rota whereby an article is written by the firm each month on say, a new case or piece of legislation.

With twelve people, for example, this only means one article a year which isn very little commitment for much greater reward.

Books
Books are admittedly a greater commitment but not something to be avoided as an unrealistic goal. Specialisation within a particular area can be extremely valuable and once completed books can provide benefit to a practice for years into the future. One way of making the writing of a book more feasible is to set up a team of people to write it within the firm with one overall editor directing the affairs. Once you have the idea, don't be backward in coming forward with the legal publishing world - they are often looking for new book ideas and you don't have to have completed the book before they will agree to publish. Simply put together a book plan with all the chapter headings and perhaps a few lines below each. Then have a look to see which companies already publish in the area your book will be and either contact them direct or perhaps if you already know an author within that area, then you might consider asking for an introduction.

Newsletters
Newsletters are enormously useful and have the added advantage that the publishing remains wholly in your own control. Focus on what the clients want to know and not necessarily on what you want to tell them. Ultimately, make it as useful as possible. Consider also providing it by email which has the advantages both of low-cost delivery and of convenience to the client. For examples of legal newsletters provided by barristers see Law Brief Update (www.lawbriefupdate.com), Medico Legal Brief Update (www.medicolegalbriefupdate.com) and Employment Law (UK) Mailing List (www.danielbarnett.co.uk).

Wider media
Related to writing is the issue of wider public relations. At the very least have people in your office monitor and build relationships with the trade press for your potential clients. Nurture also any radio and television contacts you may build up through your work. If you are accessible and put the effort in when journalists

have a tight deadline they will come to you when you are wanting to give a comment on a ground-breaking piece of new legislation.

Website

It's pretty much accepted now that if you are not online for many potential clients it's almost as if you don't exist. Make sure that you get the web-site done professionally. Shop around not only on cost of websites but on the types of sites which are being offered as there is so much variety. Avoid too many complicated frills if possible and keep the message and content clear. Once you're up and running, make sure you keep the site up to date with all the latest news and developments. Treat it as if it were the first thing that clients will see about your business. Also, remember that the overall design of the site itself will sometimes need re-doing. Something that seemed ahead of the game a few years ago can eventually start to look tired.

Search engines

These days it's not only important to have a presence on the web but also on the major search engines. Remember, even if you are recommended to a potential client, the likelihood is that they will check you out by putting your name through one of these engines and they may be onto the next firm on the list if you don't come up. Search engines are notoriously secretive as to what factors they take into account when deciding the rankings for their site. However, it will probably be possible to get advice on improving your search engine scores from the people who design your web-site. A useful site for counting the number of visitors to your site is www.sitemeter.com. The site Alexa (www.alexa.com) will tell you whether you are in the top few million websites in the world and if so, where.

It's also worth knowing that many search engines look for what are called meta-tags which are key words hidden inside many web-sites indicating what they cover. Make sure these cover all the search words you are aiming at. Another factor can be the number of links that a particular web-site has to itself and therefore it can be useful to ask people to put your link on their own site.

Be aware that you can also join up to Google and other search engines' sponsored links programmes. These are often over-looked in a marketing strategy and yet they can be very good value for money.

Blogging

Another part of modern marketing is through the use of web logs or blogs. These are basically online journals which tend to be more informal than standard websites. They allow the character of a business to come through if done well. In order to set one of these up, one of the easiest ways is simply to join one of the established providers such as www.blogger.com. After that, make sure that the blog is updated regularly.

Beyond that, it is worth over time contacting other bloggers in your field and asking them if they would consider swapping links with your own. Be aware also there are community sites dedicated to assisting bloggers such as My Blog Log (www.mybloglog.com) and Technorati (www.technorati.com).

Podcasting

Podcasting is just a technical name for putting online an audio or video file which people can then download and watch. It gets its name from Apple's iPod and is another way which firms can consider marketing themselves as part of their online strategy.

Sharing the work

One of the newest developments in the internet is the involvement of the users of content in its provision. The classic example of this is Wikipedia (http://en.wikipedia.org) an online encyclopaedia that let's its readers add to its content. So, too, You Tube (www.youtube.com) which allows readers to share videos.

Communities

Finally, consider whether there are any active communities in your area of work. There are big sites such as My Space (www.myspace.com) but there may also be smaller ones dedicated your particular type of business which it is worth considering.

Inspirations: Edith Cavell

Edith Louisa Cavell (1865 – 1915) was born in Norfolk, and trained as a nurse. During World War I she worked as a nurse for the Red Cross and courageously helped hundreds of soldiers from the allied forces escape from occupied Belgium to the neutral Netherlands. In 1915, she was arrested by the Germans for this offence. She made no defense admitting her actions, and was sentenced to death. She was executed by firing squad and became a martyr; she rightfully entered British history as a heroine.

Quotation from Edith Cavell:

The night before her execution she told the Anglican chaplain:

Patriotism is not enough, I must have no hatred or bitterness towards anyone.

These words are inscribed on her statue in St. Martin's Place, near Trafalgar Square in London

PART IV

WORK/LIFE BALANCE

Deep peace of the running wave to you.
Deep peace of the flowing air to you.
Deep peace of the quiet earth to you.
Deep peace of the shining stars to you.
Deep peace of the Son of peace to you.
Celtic blessing from the Iona Community

A.A.Milne wrote "Once upon a time, a very long time ago now, perhaps last Friday..." This has perhaps never seemed more apt than at the present, where the pace of both technological and social change is almost exponential. The digital revolution means that we are now bombarded with information and contacts from all over the world. Much of this is extremely positive and makes the world a smaller place. However, there is also a tendency towards information overload and the need to take a step back. We are also faced with the paradoxical situation that even though technology is meant to be making our lives easier and saving us time, many of us are working longer hours than ever.

It is with all of this in mind that this section on work/life balance is written. It is split into health, leisure and environment but it is recognised also that these distinctions are artificial and that there is overlap between all three. Whilst none of the suggestions promise any panacea, it is hoped that there may be some useful suggestions that might lead to small positive changes and also that some of the ideas might trigger and inspire further thoughts.

Chapter 16

HEALTH

Get in and wrestle with the sea; wing your heels with the skill and power that reside in you; bit the sea's breakers, master them and ride upon their backs as a king should.

Jack London

Introduction

Benjamin Disraeli said that "The health of the people is really a foundation upon which all their happiness and all their powers as a state depend." This applies as much to surfers as it does to lawyers and anyone else and although it is obvious in itself, it is something which is often overlooked, particularly when work life becomes particularly hectic. As with many of the issues raised in this book, there are numerous guides to particular types of health and it is not intended here to cover everything. Instead, we focus on three key constituents of health which sometimes get out of balance: sleep, food and exercise. Whilst it is hard to generalise, these are things which surfers very often tend to be better at than many people as they are absolutely key to their activities, particularly in terms of getting enough sleep to catch the early morning surf and also through the amount of exercise they get in surfing itself (described as "the seahab effect" by Allan Weisbecker in *In Search of Captain Zero*).

Sleep

Perhaps one of the most neglected aspects of health by lawyers is that of sleep. Blakemore said this about sleep, "For all the advances of modern society, we cannot afford to ignore the rhythms of the animal brain within us, any more than we can neglect our need to breathe or eat."

Most animals have a *circadian rhythm*, a cycle of various physiological and behavioural functions, synchronised to just under a twenty-five hour cycle. Even the body's immune system changes during waking and sleeping, with more *natural killer cells* present during the day and more T cells active at night. Disruptions of this pattern can explain why infections tend to plague shift-workers. The body's internal clock is about as reliable and regular as most manufactured clocks and it is thought that the body clock is located in a tiny cluster of neurons called the *suprachiasmatic nucleus (SCN)*.

How much sleep is needed?
According to Maas, the prehistoric genetic blueprint for sleep has not evolved fast enough to keep up with the pace of twenty-first century living. Humans are more likely to need an average of ten hours sleep a night rather than the four hours on which Margaret Thatcher was famously able to get by. Maas also claims that everyone maintains a personal sleep bank account, and as a rule of thumb for every two waking hours incurs a sleep debt of around one hour is incurred. Maas and others argue that modern society is a sleep-deprived society and notes that over the past twenty years an extra month of working hours has been added to the annual working and commuting time. In fact, the British work longer hours than any other nation in Europe, and sleep one-and-a-half hours less per night than two generations ago. This is not to say that everyone needs ten hours of sleep a night, or that people cannot survive on much less. However, it does raise the question that you may not have addressed, as to whether you are getting too little sleep for your own body.

Affect on health
The short answer as to whether sleep deprivation affects health is 'yes'. Sleep is important to memory, health and general well being. Further, there is a school of thought that believes that most of us carry a large 'sleep debt' and this has been linked to high blood pressure, heart attacks and strokes. Sleep debt is dangerous and

can potentially be lethal. A common example is that of road accidents are sometimes caused through tiredness. An even more extreme example is that of the Challenger space shuttle disaster, the explosion was attributed to human error caused by extreme sleep deprivation.

Sleep physiology

Sleep can be defined in terms of brain activity. When falling asleep there is a decrease in fast wave brain activity and increase in slow wave brain activity. Sleep itself is composed of five stages. The first two are the drifting off to sleep, stages three and four are slow wave sleep and finally stage five which has brain activity similar to the waking brain recording. Stage five is characterised by rapid eye movements (REM) with the eyeballs moving back and forth, up and down together under the closed lids. However, although the brain is active in REM sleep the body is not and it is characterised by muscular paralysis. The total amount of time spent in REM sleep during an average night is around ninety minutes, or 20% of the total sleep period and it is this REM stage of sleep that is thought to be most important.

Exercise –Early Bird or Night Owl?

Larks are morning types who wake early ready to face the day, whilst owls struggle to wake but stay up later at night. There is some evidence that owls' circadian rhythms are longer than twenty-four hours, while the larks' cycle is much closer to the twenty-four hours. The larks tend to endure the punishing schedule of shift work slightly better, as their internal clock remains constant even whilst working shifts. Overall though, working during the daytime is best for all types as humans are designed to be daytime species.

Lawyers are particularly prone to working long hours and mistreating their body clocks. However, even if they work regular office hours, they can still harm it at the weekend without even realising. An innocent lie-in can push the body clock forwards and come the start of the week, the 'Monday morning blues' can set in. When the alarm clock goes off earlier than the internal rhythm dictates, this is likely to culminate in feeling irritable and generally fed up.

Sleep Hygiene
The following lists give tips which should help to keep a healthy body clock.

1. Getting Ready For Bed

   a. *Develop a routine before bedtime,* so your body can learn that this process means it is time to relax and stop thinking about work or other worries. Perhaps drink a glass of milk.
   b. *Don't take your worries to bed.* Leave your worries about job and daily life behind as you get ready to go to bed. Some people find it useful to assign a "worry period" during the evening or late afternoon to deal with their issues.
   c. *Light snacks before bed.* Warm milk and foods high in the amino acid tryptophan, such as bananas, may help you to sleep.
   d. *Practice relaxation techniques before bed.* Relaxation techniques such as those mentioned in chapter 17 may help relieve anxiety and reduce muscle tension.
   e. *Establish a pre-sleep ritual.* Pre-sleep rituals, such as a warm bath or a few minutes of reading, can help you sleep. Don't watch TV as this can be engaging and keep you awake.

2. Sleep Time

   a. *Routine* - Fix a regular bedtime and awakening time. Do not allow bedtime and awakening time to drift, as the body "gets used" to falling asleep at a certain time.

   b. *Avoid alcohol 4-6 hours before bedtime.* It is common to believe that alcohol helps with sleep. However, whilst alcohol has an immediate sleep-inducing effect, a few hours later as the alcohol levels in your blood start to fall with a resulting wake-up effect, leading to disrupted sleep.

c. *Avoid caffeine 4-6 hours before bedtime.* Caffeine acts as a stimulant and is contained in many foods, such as chocolate. Food and drinks containing caffeine should be avoided before bed.

d. *Exercise - but not right before bed.* Regular exercise, particularly in the afternoon, can help sleep. But don't exercise within the two hours before bedtime as this can decrease the ability to fall asleep.

3. Sleeping Environment

a. *Bedding.* Make your bedding as comfortable as possible. Also find a comfortable temperature setting and keep the room ventilated.

b. *Eliminate as much light as possible.* This will help your brain understand it is night time and help with the sleep process.

c. *Block out all distracting noise.* This will reduce the chances of being disturbed.

d. *Reserve the bedroom.* Never use the bedroom as an office or a place of work. Let your body "know" that the bedroom is associated with sleeping.

If you find that you wake up during the night and cannot get back to sleep within fifteen to twenty minutes, then do not remain in the bed "trying hard" to sleep. Get out of bed. Leave the bedroom. Read, have a light snack, do some quiet activity, or take a bath. You will generally find that you will be able to get back to sleep twenty minutes or so later, but do not perform challenging or engaging activities whilst you are awake.

Food

Who has time to think about what they're eating? With the increasing pressures of work, family and other commitments, lawyers can easily overlook a healthy diet. In the hurried days, it can seem difficult to make the best food choices. However, it is possible to meet the demands of busy lives and still make healthy food choices.

Balance

There is no single type of balanced diet, with a fixed amount of fat, carbohydrate and protein, which suits everyone. Also, tastes and digestive preferences vary considerably. Thus a healthy diet may take a variety of different forms with differing proportions of fat, protein and carbohydrate. Focus on the nutrional quality of the food. For example, choose less-processed foods (e.g. oats) rather than highly processed alternatives (e.g. regular breakfast cereal). Choose whole grain carbs (e.g. wholegrain rye bread) rather than refined versions (e.g. fluffy white bread). Choose extra low fat ground beef/steak, rather than fattier alternatives. Choose unrefined or extra virgin vegetable oils, rather than the refined brands. Choose foods that require a little cooking, rather than instant foods.

Fruit and vegetables

Eating fruit and vegetables as part of a low-fat, high-fibre diet may help reduce blood pressure, manage weight, and reduce risk of heart disease, stroke, diabetes, and cancer. The reason for this is that they are packed with vitamins, minerals, antioxidants and fibre and are easier to absorb than nutrients from, for example, vitamin tablets. The recommended daily amounts vary, depending on age, sex, and physical activity level. The Food and Standards agency suggest, as a rule of thumb, eating 'five a day' portions of vegetables and/or fruit each day.

Salt

Always try not to intake more salt and sodium than the recommended amount (2.4 grams of sodium a day). That equals 6 grams (about 1 teaspoon) of table salt a day. The 6 grams include all salt and sodium consumed, including that used in cooking and at the table. Lower-sodium diets can help keep blood pressure from rising and help blood pressure medicines work better.

Stock up beforehand

As part of your regular routine, try to buy in the healthier foods such as fruit and vegetables. Everyone knows that it can be hard to choose grapes over crisps for a snack. However, if you only have healthy food around, the choice becomes easier. Studies show that households that have fruits and vegetables available for meals and snacks will eat more of them.

Choose healthy alternatives

Another easy way to make a healthy change is to ask for a healthy alternative when you pop out to the café. Get the 100% fruit juice rather than a coffee and a biscuit. Alternatively, make your own smoothie in the morning and take it to work with you. Low-fat yogurt, fruit juice, and fresh, canned, or frozen fruit can be used to very quickly blend into a quick smoothie.

Exercise

Exercise in general is not only good for your body, but it can also make you feel better emotionally. Exercising causes the body to produce endorphins, chemicals that produce a happy feeling. Exercise can also help some people sleep better and help with mental health, such as, mild depression and low self-esteem. The three components to a well-balanced exercise routine include aerobic exercise, strength training, and flexibility training. But often daily routine habits are great forms of exercise, such as surfing or walking the dog.

Aerobic Exercise

The heart is a muscle and it is the most important muscle to exercise. Aerobic exercise is any type of exercise that gets the heart pumping and the muscles using oxygen. When the heart gets this kind of workout on a regular basis it gets stronger and more efficient in delivering oxygen to all parts of the body. It is recommended to try and complete three twenty-minute sessions (at least) a week of vigorous activity. Surfing is a great form of aerobic exercise as it includes swimming, paddling and usually lasts well in excess of twenty minutes.

Strength Training
The heart isn't the only muscle to benefit from regular exercise - most of the other muscles in your body enjoy exercise, too. When muscles are used they become stronger, and allows them to be active for longer periods of time without getting worn out. Strong muscles are an added benefit as they actually help protect joints against injuries. For women especially exercise can prevent against osteoporosis (a weakening of the bones) as they get older. Studies have found that weight-bearing exercise, like running or brisk walking, can help keep their bones strong.

Flexibility Training
Exercise also helps the body stay flexible, meaning that muscles and joints stretch and bend easily. People who are flexible can worry less about strained muscles and sprains.

Too Much of a Good Thing
Like all good things, it's possible to overdose on exercise. Although exercising is a great way to maintain a healthy weight, exercising too much to lose weight isn't healthy. The body needs enough calories to function properly. Muscle burns more energy even at rest than fat does, so building up muscles means that more calories are needed to maintain a healthy weight.

Drugs and Alcohol
It is known that drugs such as cannabis, cocaine, amphetamines, ecstasy, LSD and heroin in some people can precipitate an acute mental illness, as well as dependency. Of course, some people who develop a psychotic illness following drug abuse had precursor symptoms of a psychotic illness, and were trying to self-medicate with drugs, which led to an exacerbation of the illness, and sometimes schizophrenia.

Whilst talking of mental health preservation it is also worth briefly discussing alcohol. With alcohol consumption increasing in some age groups and pubs being open longer hours it is important to be constantly vigilant to vulnerabilities of alcohol dependence. One way of preventing this is to try and ensure at least two or three days a week are completely alcohol free. Another useful alcohol indicator is to ask the CAGE questionnaire:

Have you ever tried to Cut down on your drinking?
Have you ever got Annoyed because someone mentioned your drinking?
Have you ever felt Guilty about the amount you are drinking?
Have you ever started to drink Early in the morning?

Inspirations: Joseph Lister – the battle against bacteria
Following the discovery of anaesthetics, one thing remained terribly wrong with surgery. Around 50% of post-operative wounds became infected; in a few days patients died after the whole blood stream became poisoned. Even the simplest operations, such as lancing an abscess would prove fatal. It did not matter how skilful the surgeon, if infection took hold the patient died. In a Glasgow hospital, a brilliant young surgeon named Joseph Lister dedicated his life to fighting this evil. Lister was the son of a Quaker family, an earnest, unassuming and deeply religious man, uninterested in social success or financial reward. Lister did not accept the school of thought that wounds became infected by some mystery gas in the air. He suspected that minute organisms entered wounds. As a meticulous researcher and surgeon, Lister recognized the relationship between Pasteur's research and his own. He considered that microbes were the likely cause of the wound putrefaction and they had to be destroyed before they entered the wound.

Lister introduced carbolic, a by-product of coal-tar, into the hospital wards and operating room. He dipped his instruments in it, and his swabs and bandages were rinsed in it. He even sprayed the air around with a fine mist of carbolic while he performed his operations. Using this new technique he found that even terrible fractures and gaping wounds, which inevitably would have become septic under the old treatment, healed in the wards under his control. Lister's techniques have since evolved into the aseptic techniques of modern surgery with steam-sterilised overalls, caps, masks and rubber gloves; perfectly sterilised instruments, operating tables, and theatres which have taken the place of the old germ-infected operating rooms.

Quotations from Joseph Lister

A feeling heart is the first requisite of a surgeon.

It is the main object of my life to find out how to procure such a result in all wounds.

Chapter 17

LEISURE

Those who go down to the sea...who perform tasks in mighty waters, they saw the works of the Lord and His wonders in the deep.

Bible, Psalm 107

Introduction

In an interview with the *Daily Telegraph*, the entrepreneur Richard Farleigh, of Dragon's Den fame explained why he divided his time 50:50 between his work and family by mentioning the story of the fisherman who fishes in the morning and spends the afternoon with his family. When an investment banker comes along and tells him to get a second boat and earn more money, the fisherman asks why, to which the banker replies, "Well, then you could relax a bit and spend more time with your family".

While his wealth obviously puts him in a privileged position, the general point he is making could apply to all. Work to live or live to work. Hopefully, it's neither and you can find work which inspires you as much as your leisure. But whether you have found that or not, it's important to prioritise breaks from work, and lawyers as a group are perhaps one of the worst groups for doing so. Clearly how to utilise leisure time to create happiness is wholly subjective. This chapter goes no further than to suggest that many of us might benefit from being a little closer to nature and having a little more solitude in our lives. It then finishes with a brief guide as to how to start surfing for those who might be interested in using their leisure time in this way. Above all, it echoes the sentiment of the famous poem by W.H. Davies entitled *Leisure*, when it says, "What is this life if full of care, / We have no time to stand and stare?"

Ideas of happiness
In *That Oceanic Feeling*, Fiona Capp reports a conversation she had with Cambridge don and author of surf books *Walking on Water* and *Stealing the Wave*, Andy Martin. In particular, he had been explaining how the modern concept of happiness had its origins in the discovery of Polynesian culture in the eighteenth century. She reports him as saying, "Happiness, le bonheur, was a universal human right for the revolutionaries. Reports about Tahiti...gave the idea of paradise substance." The contrast between this and the life back in France in his view "underlay the French revolution."

It is often this hedonistic view of happiness which still unsettles people in modern times, and which has skewed much of modern society's view. Yet happiness is in fact in the small things in our lives. The routines and the familiar. It is the contact with family and friends, the sharing of our time and our experiences and not forgetting to appreciate the simple things in life. Some might highlight evolutionary factors in this respect, forged down the generations. For example, in *On Whales*, Roger Payne suggests that the sensation of being happy, "must have been triggered for thousands of generations by very simple things...that were common to the lives of ancestors...things like good health, enough food...or a sense of well-being that comes from being surrounded by troop mates..."

Nature
The sociologist Max Weber described the breakdown of social norms and values when Europe moved from a rural to an industrial society. Its people were uprooted and transformed from family units to alienated individuals fending for themselves in the big cities. He called this phenomenon *anomie*. This may lead on to a reason why many people have a strong connection between happiness and nature in all its wildness. A return back to the simplicity of rural ways. Community. Perhaps it is simply the

escape from the noise of the town. St. Exubery said of flying that "it releases [one's] mind from the tyranny of petty things." Some might simply say that to look at nature's beauty is to experience a revelation of God. Anne Morrow Lindbergh in *Gift from the Sea* describes how it can clear the head of one's worldly woes, "Rollers on the beach, wind in the pines, the slow flapping of herons across sand dunes...One becomes...flattened by the sea; bare, open, empty as the beach, erased by today's tides of all yesterday's scribblings."

A phrase often used is that of feeding the soul. When looking out to sea, the connection can be almost visceral. Like the filling up of a spiritual tank. In *On Whales*, Roger Payne describes it as "a sort of celestial phlogiston, which ... restores souls and sets minds straight." This he compares to city dwellers whose disconnection with nature has drained them of this goodness to the point of what he calls urbanicide, "until they are a hollow husk of the full ripe ear of their pastoral ancestors".

Silence
Along with nature, silence can also be an important factor which is often missing from busy modern lives. In *Gift from the Sea*, Anne Morrow Lindbergh describes all the demands of modern life. In particular, the following words probably have particular resonance for lawyers, "Not knowing how to feed the spirit, we try to muffle its demands in distractions. Instead of stilling the center, the axis of the wheel, we add more centrifugal activities to our lives — which tend to throw us off balance."

She describes the solution as "neither in total renunciation of the world, nor in total acceptance of it" and that the balance was "a swinging of the pendulum between solitude and communion, between retreat and return". As part of that balance, the solitude was to be found for her by the ocean. As part of the exercise of silence, the words of Rainer Maria Rilke in *Letters to a Young Poet* assist, "Be patient toward all that is unsolved in your heart and try to love the questions...Do not seek the answers, which cannot be given to you because you would not be able to live them." The point he went on was to live the questions until you "gradually without noticing it, live your way some distant day into the answer."

In *Finding Sanctuary*, Abbot Christopher Jamison explains the Rule of St Benedict and the need for silence in one's life. The Rule says in particular that "There are times when good words are to be left unsaid out of esteem for silence." However, he also describes the challenge of finding what he calls "positive silence" in the city, although he says perhaps the biggest challenge is to help people find positive silence inside themselves. However, he goes on that the laying of a carpet of silence is in fact only an underlay as the noises in the head remain. What is needed beyond this, he says, is what he calls "the carpet of contemplation". This, he suggests, can be done through prayer, meditation and good reading.

Relaxation

Mental relaxation
Most of us have our own method of switching off, such as music, exercise, reading, or talking to family and friends. These methods may not work so well when we are under stress, and worrying thoughts whizz through the mind in a flow that's hard to stop. In this case, visualisation may help. Set aside a quiet time, place and leave at least fifteen minutes for a session. At first you will no doubt find the visualisation techniques difficult. But if you persevere, slow your breathing a little and relax your body, you should find that you can relax into the imagined details of the pleasant scene.

'Mindfulness training' is a form of relaxation and the critical aspect of this training is that you don't use effort to keep your mind on your breathing. Rather you practise being aware of whether your mind is on your breath. When it strays away from this, rather than feeling annoyed with yourself simply draw it back to your breath in a relaxed way. Many people find that if they practice this once or twice a day for about fifteen to twenty minutes, it helps them feel more relaxed and calm.

Physical relaxation

A variation in this is to imagine that the sun is shining down on your head and slowly you feel it pass from the top of your head through every part of your body. Imagine it moving slowly through your body and as it does, relax that particular part of your body further through to your fingers and the tips of your toes.

Breathing exercises

A commonly suggested breathing exercise to increase energy and general well-being, particular when meditating or relaxing is the so-called 'four-sixteen-eight' exercise. This involves breathing in for a count of four, holding your breath for a count of sixteen and then breathing out for a count of eight. This can be done up to ten times in one go.

While you are doing this, you can also practice a further breathing exercise. As you breath in, push your stomach out and as you breath out pull your stomach in. Though to start with it may not feel particularly natural, it will actually help you to relax.

Learn to surf

In the film *Point Break*, the character Nathaniel says, "Lawyers don't surf" to which Bodhi replies "This one does". If any of you choose to try surfing for yourselves, then it is highly recommend to go through a surf school. They can teach you about safety and give you the basics before you get into the water. Check also that you are insured with them for any accidents you might cause. If you're not with a surf school, then it might be worth joining the British Surfing Association (BSA) (www.britsurf.co.uk) as they offer third party liability insurance as part of their membership. A couple of books which you might find useful are: *Surfing: A Beginner's Manual* by Wayne Alderson (Fernhurst Books, 1996) and *Surfer's Start-up: Beginner's Guide to Surfing* by Doug Werner (Tracks Publishing, 1999). There are numerous books, websites and films listed under 'Further Sources' at the end of this book.

Surf etiquette

Whilst surfing is not generally associated with rules, there are a number of basic standards that all surfers adhere to, mostly for their own safety. The BSA website has a code of conduct which is well worth reading before going out. Here are a few pointers:

1. The most important rule in surfing is that the surfer closest to the peak should have the wave. If someone else is closer, you must not in any circumstances 'drop in' on them. Not only is it dangerous but it is also likely to get you shouted out of the sea.

2. Respect the locals in particular. The seas don't belong to anyone but they've been waiting around longer for these waves than you.

3. In the same vein, don't queue jump. If someone is nearer to the oncoming wave than you, don't rush over and paddle round them just to get priority. This is called snaking.

4. Nor should you try and hog the waves. Instead, be generous and share. There will always be another wave coming along.

5. Do not paddle out through the line up or the impact zone and do not paddle behind other surfers. Paddle around.

6. Do not paddle in front of or across the path of a surfer who is already riding a wave.

7. Keep control of your equipment.

8. Always watch out for others who might be in trouble.

9. Don't surf alone.

Tips for surfing

As well the rules, the following provide a number of tips which you might find useful when starting out:

1. When deciding what day to go, remember that off-shore winds (from the land to the sea) are best or no wind at all. On-shore winds tend to turn the sea into a mush of white water. Check that there is likely at least

to be some waves. A very good forecasting site for wind and well is www.magicseaweed.com.

2. When starting out, go to beach breaks where the only thing you can get thrown onto is a sandy bottom. Stay well clear of rocks.

3. Make sure you get a longish board (7'6" or above). Short boards may look cool but they won't when you're continually failing to catch any waves.

4. Before putting your foot into your wetsuit to get it on, put a plastic carrier bag over your foot. It will help it slide through far more easily.

5. If it's hot remember waterproof sun-block.

6. Also, if it's very hot, make sure you have warm water wax on your board which melts at higher temperatures. Otherwise you'll be slipping all over the place.

7. Don't surf if you've been drinking alcohol. Also, give yourself a fair time after eating.

8. Before you paddle out, have a careful look at the sea and look for rip currents and channels. These are very common and you need to be very careful with these. However, note that sometimes a current out to sea can help you paddle safely out the back.

9. Check that the sea is safe. Watch out for warning flags and don't go in if the waves are too bog big for your experience. If in any doubt, ask someone.

10. Time your entry into the sea so that it is just after a set has passed to give you some time to get out before the next set.

11. If you get caught in a rip, paddle across it diagonally and towards the shore.

12. Always keep on your leash which attaches to your board.

13. When you're looking for the right place to wait for waves, look where the last wave broke and paddle over to the back of the white water foam which it leaves behind in its wake. This can often be a good indicator for where the next wave might also break.

14. Once you've found the right spot to wait for a wave, take a bearing. Line-up two points to your left and

right and also one on front of you. This will help you find that spot again after you've caught a wave in. It's also why they call the place where people wait the "lineup".

15.   When you go for a wave make sure you commit and always try and jump to your feet as soon as possible.

16.   After surfing, don't leave your board lying around in the sun as it may discolour and lose its shape. If you have to leave it out, make sure it is the top side down so that the wax doesn't melt so fast. Don't clean it with hot water either.

17.   The same goes for wetsuits as they can harden and crack.

18.   If you're in a country with sharks try and stay where there are shark nets. Even then, these do not guarantee against sharks and avoid surfing at the high risk times of sunrise and sunset.

19.   Don't carry on surfing once it starts getting dark.

20.   Take your litter home with you.

Inspirations: Jean Jacques Rousseau - The Rights of Man

Jean Rousseau (1712-1778) was born in Geneva, Switzerland. His mother died nine days after his birth due to complications from childbirth, and his father, a watchmaker, abandoned him to avoid imprisonment for fighting a duel. In his childhood, Rousseau often read in the tranquility of a garden, which he would later describe as the most serene part of growing up.

Rousseau saw a fundamental divide between *society* and *human nature* and contended that *man* was good by nature, but corrupted by society. Perhaps his most influential work was *The Social Contract*. It gave the world ideas about the natural rights of everyman and analysed the whole question of government; and who should benefit from it. His answer was the common man. Some claim that his influences instigated the French Revolution.

His writings made startling changes as he put his beliefs about liberty, equality, and democracy into words. As a result he was heard as a trumpet call, and people all round the world rallied to this brave new standard.

Quotations from Rousseau

Liberty, Equality and Fraternity.

It is the common people who make up the human race. What is not the common people is hardly worth considering.

In the state of nature equality is a real and inviolable fact.

Chapter 18

ENVIRONMENT

To stand at the edge of the sea, to sense the ebb and flow of the tides, to feel the breath of a mist moving over a great salt marsh, to watch the flight of shore birds that have swept up and down the surf lines of the continents for untold thousands of year, to see the running of the old eels and the young shad to the sea, is to have knowledge of things that are as nearly eternal as any earthly life can be.

Rachel Carson

Introduction

'Time and tide wait for no man' as the saying goes. First ascribed to Chaucer, the word tide meant 'time' in those days. However, today it applies equally to the ebb and flow of the sea and resonates powerfully in these times of environmental need. The consequences of the damage and the rise of the sea flow as inevitably as the tide and all we can hope is that the world reacts in time.

Surfers' connection with the environment comes primarily from the fact that they spend so many hours staring out on its vastness. Contemplating its forces. Harnessing its power. As Matt Warshaw says in *Maverick's: The Story of Big-Wave Surfing*, "Surfing expresses ... a pure yearning for visceral, physical contact with the natural world." However, perhaps it's something more than this. Taking a perspective from a breaking wave. In geometry, mathematicians describe a straight line which touches the edge of a curve at a particular point as a tangent. Perhaps the surfboard is the tangent on the edge of the world. In *Caught Inside*, Daniel

Daune talks about the Ohlone, the indigenous people of Northern California who have lived in California for over 1,500 years and quotes a line from their which has survived and which he says, "makes perfect sense to me as I surf here before so much space: dancing on the brink of the world."

Dancing on the brink of the world. The surfer as the point of intersection between the world and the tangent line of the surfboard. The surfer balancing on the top of the world. Surveying all before him. Perhaps there is even more. Surfers not only standing on top of the world but also at the intersection of the land and the sea as well as that between the sea and the sky. In *That Oceanic Feeling*, Fiona Capp said that she was "Entranced by that mythical line where the sea meets the sky, Tennyson's Ulysses regarded all experience as 'an arch wherethrough gleams that untravelled world whose margin fades for ever and for ever when I move'."

Surfers standing at the intersection of the world. The portal or meeting place of nature's forces. Maybe it's all or none of these things. Whatever it is, there's an essence which continues to elude just as when we grasp at the ocean we are left only with its salty residue. Yet for all that we may romanticize nature, we must never forget its dangers, increasingly evident in the environmental disasters which are hitting our planet. In *Cannery Row*, John Steinbeck points to the dangers of turning a blind eye to nature's primeval forces, "Here a crab tears a leg from his brother...Then the creeping murderer the octopus, steals out, slowly, softly, moving like a gray mist, pretending to be a bit of weed, now a rock, now a lump of decaying meat while its evil goat eyes watch coldly."

It is the shadow to the light. A reminder of nature's harsh realities. Just as the crab tears the leg in the microcosm of the ocean so a hurricane can tear away a city. It is something which can affect us all and for which we are all responsible. Not just a problem which others need to solve. Surfers as much as anyone else. They drive many miles to the ocean, often in large vans or with a board on their roof adding to their carbon footprint. They fly all over the world in search of waves and when they get there they put on wetsuits and paddle out on boards which cannot be recycled.

This chapter does not seek to explain or break down all of the various scientific and other studies on the environment. Instead, it first of all looks at the need for inspiration in respect of our collective view of the environment and then goes on to look at a small number of the things which we might all be able to do to help the environment around us.

Inspiration

W.H. Auden famously observed in his elegy 'In Memory of W.B. Yeats' that "poetry makes nothing happen." However, despite this negative perspective, art in all its forms retains an ability to inspire the mind, providing images which enter us and grow through the nurturing of our own thoughts and experiences.

This was so as far back as 1789 when Rev Gilbert White wrote *The Natural History and Antiquities of Selborne*. So, too, the following century with Herman Melville's *Moby Dick* with its vivid descriptions of the sea and the mighty forces of the natural world. One of the first writers positively to rail against human destruction of the environment was the poet Gerard Manley Hopkins, lamenting in *Binsey Poplars*, "O if we but knew what we do / When we delve or hew – / Hack and rack the growing green!" So, too, in *God's Grandeur* he wrote, "Generations have trod, have trod, have trod, / And all is seared with trade; bleared, smeared with soil / Is bare now, nor can foot feel, being shod."

Another writer who had a profound effect in the way we view the world was scientist turned writer Rachel Carson with her books which included *The Edge of the Sea* (1955) and later *The Silent Spring* (1962) which eventually led to the ban of the pesticide DDT in the United States. More recently, there has been in particular Carl Safina with *Song for the Blue Ocean* (1998), *Eye of the Albatros* (2002) and *Voyage of the Turtle* (2006) and David Helvarg with *Blue Frontier – Saving America's Living Seas* (2001). Another person who has deeply affected the way we perceive nature is Roger Payne, who is best known for his discovery (with

Scott McVay) that humpback whales sing songs. He helped record
the whale songs which were put aboard the spacecraft *Voyager* as
evidence of intelligent life on Earth and has also written beautifully
about whales and the environment in *Among Whales* (1995).

As with the sound of the whale, so with the visual image of the
Earth and the best example of this is a photograph taken by the
crew of the Apollo 17 spacecraft in 1972 which was the first clear
image of an illuminated face of the Earth. It has been nicknamed
"The Blue Marble" after its similarity to the appearance of a
child's glass marble. It has been credited as providing the human
race with a real perspective as to the size and vulnerability of the
Earth in relation to the vast expanse of space.

All of these are examples of how art in all its forms, not only
affects us but ultimately may help to inspire solutions. Perhaps
above all, they break down the barriers we have built up between
us and the environment around us, make us realise that we are all
connected. As Chief Seattle of Nez Perce is reported to have said in
1884, "What happens to beasts will happen to man. All things are
connected. If the great beasts are gone, man would surely die of a
great loneliness of spirit."

We can all make a difference
The problem in dealing with the environment is that the issues are
so big as to be overwhelming and can lead people to conclude that
we are unable to have any effect. However, as Edmund Burke said,
"No one could make a greater mistake than he who did nothing
because he could do only a little." We can all make a difference
not only through the effect of our own actions on the environment
around us but also by the intangible effect of our own actions
potentially inspiring others.

Both of these effects are illustrated by the story of Robin Kevan at
the end of this chapter and by the numerous other examples of
people who simply decided to get on and do something rather than
sitting around wringing one's hands over the situation. An
inspiring book in this respect is *The Man Who Planted Trees* by
Jean Giono which is an allegorical tale about a shepherd's single-

handed effort to re-forest a valley in the foothills of the Alps. Over forty years, simply by planting trees, he turns it from a desolate landscape to a peacefully settled and vibrant ecosystem. An animated adaptation of the story was produced by Frédéric Back in 1987, going on to win an Academy Award for best animated short film.

As to the question as to whether the world as a whole is able to make a difference to the environment, the best example is the way the destruction of the ozone layer by CFCs was turned around in the 1980s and 1990s following the original discovery of the hole in the ozone layer by a British Antarctic expedition in the 1970s.

Action by individuals
We are constantly bombarded with ideas as to how to help the environment and often it's hard to boil them down into some simple practical steps. Here are a few suggestions which are commonly made:

1. Drive less and keep your tyres inflated for better fuel efficiency.
2. Re-cycle where you can.
3. Use less electricity energy by adjusting the thermostat, changing to energy-saving light bulbs, and considering low-flow showerheads and washing clothes in warm as opposed to hot water.
4. Save electricity by turning off electrical devices such as your TV, DVD player, stereo and computer when you're not using them.
5. Avoid products with a lot of packaging.
6. Consider moving to a green electricity provider such as one which uses wind power as opposed to fossil fuels in its processes.
7. Consider off-setting either some of or all of your emissions through, for example, joining a scheme which plants trees in proportion to your carbon footprint.

Action by business

In *Let My People Go Surfing: The Education of a Reluctant Businessman* (2005), Yvon Chouinard, the founder of the outdoor clothing company, Patagonia, describes his path towards eventually becoming a businessman and how he created a company which was both environmentally and socially responsible. It is an inspiration to any aspiring businessman but particularly so for those with an interest in the environment. One of the things he emphasises is donating to good causes and describes his support for the One Per Cent for the Planet organisation, the principle being, in the words of David Brower, that, "There is no business to be done on a dead planet."

As well as considering giving money, businesses can consider how they can facilitate their staff to be more environmentally friendly. A good start is to set up a corporate social responsibility programme in which consideration can be given to all aspects of the business. Examples might include law firms organising schemes where transport needs are shared or where they decide to go paperless for as much of their work as possible. It might be that firms decide to change to a green electricity provider or simply change their systems in order to minimise energy usage. Other examples might be more imaginative, such as the use of green businesses like online CPD provider CPD Webinars (www.cpdwebinars.com).

Action by Surfers

As for surfers, there are a number of environmental groups which have come grown out of surfing, including Surfers Against Sewage, the Surfrider Foundation and Save the Waves. In addition, there have been some moves towards reducing the impact of surfing itself on the environment. Examples of this include the Eco-Board inspired by the Eden Project under the supervision of Chris Hines and the Eco-Foil boards produced by Ocean Green. In addition, numerous surf companies have taken individual stances for the environment. A particularly interesting initiative is the EcoSurf Project which has been set up to help create a sustainable, environmentally-friendly, socially responsible future for surfing and related sports.

Inspirations: Rob the Rubbish

Robin Kevan (1945-present day) was born in Yorkshire, England. He was a social worker for most of his adult life and upon retirement moved to Llanwrtyd Wells in mid-Wales. A country-lover all of his life, he wanted to do something about the environment around him and so one day he got up very early and cleaned up his little Welsh village and continued to do this most mornings, gaining the nick-name 'Rob the Rubbish'. He eventually decided to take his efforts further afield and cleaned up Ben Nevis, Mount Snowdon and Scafell Pike among others. Eventually his efforts were picked up by the media and following profiles on programmes such as *Countryfile* and *The Richard and Judy Show* someone offered to take him to the foothills of Mount Everest to clean the path to base camp. He completed this in 2006 and is now planning further projects both in the Himalayas and other remote places. One of the reasons he has inspired so many people is that he refuses to get angry about litter and instead has turned the problem on its head and made the cleaning of it a positive in his life. He has become a symbol not only for those who love the beauty of the countryside but also for what can be achieved by one man.

On the 4th of September 2006, *The Daily Telegraph* described him as "the unlikely new hero of the environmental lobby". The *Independent* stated in one of its leaders in 2005 that "Mr Kevan thus follows in the footsteps of others who have decided something must be done and done it. One thinks of Florence Nightingale, Albert Schweitzer, Bob Geldof, Diana, Princess of Wales...". At the end of 2005, Stephen Jardine of the Edinburgh Evening News stated that Robin Kevan was his choice for Man of the Year and concluded: "Britain needs more people like Rob the Rubbish who recognise enough is enough and are prepared to take responsibility for doing something about it." In December 2006 he was invited by the Prime Minister to 10 Downing Street to thank him for his contribution to the voluntary sector. He continues to keep his local village clean. He is the father of the co-author of this book, Tim Kevan. See www.robtherubbish.com.

Quotations from Rob the Rubbish

At 61 years of age, I feel I cannot wait for a generation of children to be educated in conventional ways about the litter problem. Whilst that education is taking place litter tends to stay on the ground. I decided that just maybe an equally effective way of dealing with the problem was to turn litter on its head. I decided not to be confrontational or grumpy about it but to seek to use it to mine and the wider community's advantage by picking it up. My philosophy is that once litter is gone it is no longer a problem, cannot offend any more and the beauty behind it can be seen.

I liken myself to a magic fairy who spirits away all the litter before the townsfolk get up.

My basic 'raison d'etre' is that if litter offends me and I pick it up it can no longer do so, and I can see the beauty beyond it.

PART V

CONCLUSION

Thou, O Lord, that stillest the raging of the sea, hear us, hear us, and save us, that we perish not.

Book of Common Prayer

Chapter 19

CONCLUSION

For all at last return to the sea –
To Oceanus, the ocean river.
Like the ever-flowing stream of time,
The beginning and the end.
Rachel Carson, *The Sea Around Us (1951)*

Introduction

Whether we are lawyers, doctors, accountants or from any other walk of life, perhaps we all return to our roots at some point on our journey through life. This was illustrated in Paolo Coelho's *The Alchemist*, where the hero went out in search of treasure only to find that it was in fact lying where his journey had begun: his home, his heart, ultimately, love. John F. Kennedy said, "We are tied to the ocean. And when we go back to the sea, whether it is to sail or to watch - we are going back from whence we came".

Perhaps that's the point. Just as all the rivers flow inexorably towards their ultimate source, the ocean, perhaps our lives equally flow back towards their beginnings. The meanderings along the way are all part of that journey although at the time this may not be particularly obvious. T.S.Eliot wrote in *The Four Quartets*, "In my beginning is my end... / We shall not cease from exploration / And the end of all our exploring / Will be to arrive where we started / And know the place for the first time."

The ocean as the metaphor to explore life, our relationships with each other, love, God. The ocean as a conduit. Without form and void and yet a connection to something greater, something we can only imagine in the fringes of our thoughts. The ocean as the depths of our subconscious. In *The Face of the Deep*, Thomas

Farber reminds us of what lies beneath and that, "When we look out at the vast blue, we see not ocean, exactly, but surface: master trickster, chameleon, boundary between water and atmosphere, barrier or seal between two realities."

The breaking wave as the boundary with the conscious mind, the route into the unconscious. Jung's anima and animus in one. The guide to the unconscious. The light to the shadow. Perhaps it is something to do with the timeless quality of the ocean. The fact that whilst it never remains the same, it appears on the surface to be unmarked by the ravages of time. In *Caught Inside*, Daniel Duane says that his friend Willie described surfing, "as having the quality of Japenese dancing on rice paper, in which the dancer steps so delicately that the paper never tears, and pointed out how each wave washes away all that has come before." So, mountains, valleys, living creatures. All bow to time's dominion. The ocean on the other hand appears as a constant. As Henry David Thoreau said, "We do not associate the idea of antiquity with the ocean, nor wonder how it looked a thousand year, as we do of the land, for it was equally wild and unfathomable always."

However, just because its physical appearance on the surface does not change, that is not to say that events do not take their toll and this is perhaps never more clearly illustrated than the present day when the ocean is being polluted to such an extent that many forms of sea-life are now struggling to survive. Water's memory is more subtle but no less profound. Perhaps again, a symbol of the unconscious. In *Water, Ice and Stone*, Bill Green talked about "how water retained, like a childhood memory, a trace of its past as ice. How it never forgot that. How it carried that singular fact with it...all the way to boiling point." A.R.Ammons, "The very longest swell in the ocean, I suspect, carries the deepest memory." Keats, "Wide sea, that one continuous murmur breeds along the pebbled shore of memory!"

The voice from our souls, our relationship to the world around us, the meaning of life itself. These are all issues which very often are not particularly dealt with in many of the slightly mechanical quick-fix motivational manuals. This is undoubtedly because of the difficulty of pinning down any specific causes, effects and solutions. However, to ignore the deep murmurings of the soul is to turn away from life itself, just as it is to turn away from the sea. Edith Sitwell once wrote, "What are you staring at, mariner man /Wrinkled as sea-sand and old as the sea?"

Go visit the sea.

Look out on its ever-changing mass and wonder.

Maybe even consider paddling out.

Then look far out the back and reflect.

As surfers do.

Time's Dominion

Mountain,
silent warrior,
bearing time's scars
in its noble crags.

Ocean,
mountain's mirror,
refusing time's ravage,
without form and void.

Mountain,
decayed, honest,
embracing time
with dignity.

Ocean,
time's unconscious,
internalising
polluted memories.

Tide,
ocean's heartbeat
on the shoreline,
outside of time.

Mountain,
living.

Ocean,
dying.

Its soul unfurling
to time's dominion.

FURTHER SOURCES

Without books the development of civilisation would have been impossible. They are the engines of change, windows on the world, "Lighthouses" as the poet said "erected in the sea of time".

Arthur Shopenhauer

SURFING-RELATED

Surf books

Adams, Dawnea, *Soul Surfing* (Dell, 1999)
Alderson, Wayne, *Surfing: A Beginner's Manual* by Wayne Alderson (Fernhurst Books, 1996)
Alderson, Wayne, Surfing UK (Fernhurst)
Anderson, Tom, Riding the Magic Carpet (2006)
Blake, Tom, Voice of the Wave (1968, reprinted, Surfer's Journal, Vol 8,3)
Butt, Tony and Russel, Paul, Surf Science
Bystrom, Chris, *The Glide* (Duranbah Press, 1998)
Canfield, Jack; Hansen, Mark Victor; Wyland; Creech, Steve; *Chicken Soup for the Ocean Lover's Soul* (Health Communications, 2003)
Capp, Fiona, *That Oceanic Feeling* (Aurum Press, 2004)
Carroll, Nick, *Visions of the Breaking Wave* (Surfing Life)
Chouniard, Yvon, *Let my people go surfing* (Penguin, 2005)
De La Vega, Timothy T. (orchestrated by), *200 Years of Surfing Literature* (De La Vega, 2004)
Duane, Daniel, *Caught Inside* (North Point Press, 1996)
Farber, Thomas, *On Water* (Oakeanos Press, 1991)

Farber, Thomas, *The Face of the Deep* (Mercury House, 1998)
Footprint Series for Britain, Europe and the world
Helvarg, David, *50 Ways to Save the Ocean* (Inner Ocean Publishing, 2006)
Kampion, Drew, *The Book of Waves*, (Roberts Rinehart, 1989)
Kampion, Drew; and Peterson, Jeff; *The Lost Coast*, (Gibbs Smith, 2004)
Kampion, Drew; and Peterson, Jeff; *Waves*, (Gibbs Smith, 2005)
Kotler, Steven, *West of Jesus* (Bloomsbury, 2006)
Levin, Wayne; Farber, Thomas; Carlson, Bruce A; Stewart, Frank, *other oceans* (University of Hawaii Press, 2001)
Lindbergh, Anne Morroe, *Gift from the Sea* (1955)
Long, John (editor), The Big Drop (Falcon, 1999)
Marcus, Ben, Surfing and the Meaning of Life (Voyageur Press, 2006)
Martin, Andy, Walking on Water (John Murray, 1991)
Martin, Andy, Stealing the Wave (Bloomsbury, 2007)
Melville, Herman, Moby Dick (1851)
Nunn, Kem, Dogs of Winter and *Tapping the Source*
O'Carroll, Carol and Vogan, Patty, *Surf-vival, handbook for land and sea* (Regent, 2004)
*Portugal (*Oceansurf)
Payne, Roger, Among Whales (Scribner, 1995)
Safina, Carl, *Voyage of the Turtle* (Henry Holt, 2006)
Severson, John, Modern Surfing Around the World (1964)
Shifren, Nachum, Surfing Rabbi, (Heaven Ink, 2001)
Smith, Don, *Surfing the Big Wave* (Troll,1976)
Stormrider Guides to Europe and the world
Thomson, Carl, Surfing in Great Britain (1972)
Tomson, Shaun (with Patrick Moser), Surfer's Code (Gibbs Smith, 2006)
Wade, Alex, Surf Nation (Simon & Schuster, 2007)
Wardlaw, Lee, *Cowabunga* (Avon, 1991)
Warshaw, Matt, *Zero Break* (Harcourt, 2004)
Werner, Doug, Surfer's Start-up and *Longboarder's Start-up* (Tracks Publishing).
Willis, Milton and Willis, Michael, *Discover the greatness in you* (Blue Mountain Press, 2006)

Surf websites

A1 Surf: www.a1surf.com
Alex Wade: http://alexwade.com
Blue Frontier Campaign: http://bluefront.org/news
Blue Ocean Institute: www.blueocean.org
Bron Taylor: www.religionandnature.com/bron
Christian Surfers UK: www.christiansurfers.co.uk
Croyde Surf Cam: www.croyde-surf-cam.com
Drew Kampion: www.drewkampion.com
Drift Magazine: www.driftmagazine.co.uk
EcoSurf Project: www.ecosurfproject.org
Eyeball Surf Check: www.eyeball-surfcheck.co.uk
Live Surf Cams: www.livesurfcams.co.uk
Magic Seaweed: http://magicseaweed.com
Ocean Alliance: www.oceanalliance.org
Ocean Green Surfboards: www.oceangreen.org
One Per Cent for the Planet: www.onepercentfortheplanet.org
Save the Waves: www.savethewaves.org
Surfers Against Sewage: www.sas.org.uk
Surfer's Path Magazine: www.surferspath.com
Surf GSD: www.surfgsd.com/about.asp
Surf Nation: http://timesonline.typepad.com/surf_nation
Surfrider Foundation: www.surfrider.org
Surf South West: www.surfsouthwest.com
Surf Station: www.surfstation.co.uk/report.html
Thomas Farber: www.thomasfarber.org
Tiki Surf: www.tikisurf.co.uk
Tom Anderson: www.tomandersonbooks.com
Wanna Surf: www.wannasurf.com
Wetsand: www.wetsand.com

Surf movies

Big Wednesday, Endless Summer & Endless Summer II, Riding Giants, Flow, North Shore,Point Break, Blue Crush.

MOTIVATIONAL

Andreas, Steve and Faulkner, Charles, *NLP The New Technology of Achievement* (1st edition, 1996, Nicholas Brealey Publishing)

Boon, Andy, *Advocacy* (2nd edition, 1999, Cavendish Legal Publishing)

Butler-Bowden, Tom, *50 Self-Help Classics* (1st edition, 2003, Nicholas Brealey Publishing)

Carpenter, Dr Roger, *Neurophysiology* (3rd edition, 1996, Arnold)

Campbell, Joseph, *The Hero With a Thousand Faces* (1993, Fontana)

Covey, Stephen R., *The 7 Habits of Highly Effective People* (1st edition, 1989, Simon & Schuster UK Ltd)

Cohen, Pete, *Life DIY* (1st edition, 2004, Element)

Devalia, Arvind, *Get a Life* (1st edition, 2003, Nirvana Publishing)

Evans, Keith, *The Golden Rules of Advocacy*, (1st edition, 1993, Oxford University Press)

Gross, Richard, *Psychology, The Science of Mind and Behaviour*, (4th edition, 2003, Hodder and Stoughton)

Fennell, Melanie, *Overcoming Low Self-Esteem*, (1999, Robinson Publishing)

Franklin, Bejamin, *Autobiography* (1790)

Hanley, Dr Jesse Lynn and Deville, Nancy, *Tired of Being Tired* (1st edition, 2002, Michael Joseph, Penguin)

Heppell, Michael, *How to be Brilliant* (1st edition, 2004, Pearson Education Ltd)

Hyam, Michael, *Advocacy Skills* (4th edition, 1999, Oxford University Press)

Johnson, Dr Spencer, *Who Moved My Cheese* (1st edition, 1999, Vermilion)

Lowndes, Leil, *How to Talk to Anyone* (1st edition, 1999, Thorsons)

Maister, David H., *True Professionalism* (1st edition, 2000, Touchstone)

Macmillan, Lord, *Law and Other Things* (1937, Cambridge University Press)

McKeith, Dr Gillian, *You are What You Eat* (1st edition, 2004, Michael Joseph, Penguin)

McKenna, Paul, *Change Your Life in 7 Days* (1st edition, 2004, Bantam Press)

Moore, Thomas, *Care of the Soul* (1992, Piatkus)

Munkman, John, *The Technique of Advocacy* (1st edition, 1991, Butterworths)

Pease, Allan, *Body Language* (3rd edition, 1997, Camel Publishing Co.)

Persaud, Dr Raj, *Staying Sane: How to make your mind work for you* (2001, Bantam Books)

Persaud, Dr Raj, *Simply Irresistible* (2006, Bantam Press)

Robbins, Anthony, *Awaken the Giant Within* (1st edition, 1992, Simon & Schuster Ltd)

Robbins, Anthony, *Notes from a Friend* (1st edition, 1996, Simon & Schuster Ltd)

Robbins, Anthony, *Unlimited Power* (1st edition, 1989, Simon & Schuster Ltd)

Savill, Antoinette and Hamilton, Dawn, *Super Energy Detox* (1st edition, 2002, Thorsons)

Selby, Hugh, *Winning in Court: An Introduction to Advocacy* (1st edition, 2000, Oxford University Press)

Syer, John & Connolly, Christopher, *107 Insider Ideas to Make You a Winner* (Keith News Ltd)

Templar, Richard (1st edition, 2003, Pearson Education Ltd)

Tupman, Simon, *Why Lawyers Should Eat Bananas* (1st edition, 2000, Simon Tupman Presentations Pty Ltd)

Vogler, Christopher, *The Writer's Journey* (1999, Pan)

Woods, Caspian, *From Acorns...how to build your brilliant business from scratch* (Pearson Education Ltd, 2004)

The Future of the NHS
Edited: Dr Michelle Tempest

In a book that is well written and accessible to readers, whatever their background, Dr Michelle Tempest has brought together a range of contributors that is unique.

For the first time, the views of patients, leading medics and opinion formers can be read alongside the politicians without being drowned out by spin or sound bite.

Whether you are a patient, an NHS employee, a supplier or a politician taking part in the debate is essential – this book helps you do so understanding all the issues.

Buy the paperback   www.xplpublishing.com
Join the debate   www.thefutureofthenhs.com

ACKNOWLEDGMENTS

In writing this book, we have been helped and inspired by a number of people to whom we are extremely grateful and we cannot possibly name them all here.

Friends and family
Thanks for the unconditional love and continual support of our parents and sisters. IT expert Garry Wright and barrister Daniel Barnett for their helpful suggestions; Rev Dr John Stott and Rev Bill Long for their spiritual guidance and wisdom; and our families for their love and support.

Publishing
Publisher Andrew Griffin for putting his faith in the project from the beginning and to Ben Wilson for the wonderful art work.

Professional Friends
We both owe much to our clients and patients respectively for all that they have taught us. IT expert Garry Wright and barrister Daniel Barnett for their helpful suggestions; Rev Dr John Stott and Rev Bill Long for their spiritual guidance and wisdom. We would also like to thank Dr Ivana Rosenweig, Dr Tina Malhotra, Dr Tag Uygur, Laura Davies and Dr John Keown.

Surfing and writing
All those writers mentioned within and at the back of this book and in particular Alex Wade, Thomas Farber, Andy Martin, Tom Anderson, Drew Kampion, Bron Taylor, Daniel Duane and Fiona Capp for their inspiring work; Richard and Matt Waddams, Steve Cavell, Ewan Merer, Jonny Bull and Brad Cousens for their guidance on surfing over the years; also Derek McLeod and Rodney "Cheggs" Jamieson for making us both so welcome on surf trips to the Outer Hebrides.

Tim Kevan,   Michelle Tempest,
Barrister.   Psychiatrist.